509   5.65

CE Kew

7

GUILT:
Where Religion
And
Psychology Meet

PRENTICE-HALL INTERNATIONAL, INC., *London*
PRENTICE-HALL OF AUSTRALIA, PTY., LTD., *Sydney*
PRENTICE-HALL OF CANADA, LTD., *Toronto*
PRENTICE-HALL FRANCE, S. A. R. L., *Paris*
PRENTICE-HALL OF JAPAN, INC., *Tokyo*
PRENTICE-HALL DE MEXICO, S. A., *Mexico City*

GUILT:

Where Religion
And
Psychology Meet

DAVID BELGUM, Ph.D.

Northwestern Lutheran
Theological Seminary

PRENTICE-HALL, INC. *Englewood Cliffs, N.J.*

1963

Printed in the United States of America
37161-C

To Kathie,
Wife and Companion

ACKNOWLEDGMENTS

Gratitude is hereby acknowledged to the Eli Lilly Endowment through whose generous Research Fellowship this study was made possible. In a sense the following pages are a fulfillment of their trust as well as that of my own Seminary, which graciously provided the sabbatical leave for this investigation.

Dr. O. Hobart Mowrer, Research Professor in the Psychology Department at the University of Illinois, was the stimulating and concerned mentor, who guided us in our studies of Pastoral Theology on the theme: the genesis, function, and resolution of personal guilt. I also benefited from the comradeship of the other two Fellows in the Program: Father James Harney, O. P., Saint Albert's College (Seminary), Oakland, California, and Dr. Maurice Jackson, Berkeley Baptist Divinity School, Berkeley, California. These three have been warm friends and helpful critics.

I am also indebted to the Staff of the Galesburg State Research Hospital where we three Fellows were privileged to work together with Dr. Mowrer in his unique approach to the problems of mental patients. Thanks are also due to the Psychology Department and the Psychological Clinic at the University of Illinois for hospitality and use of facilities, as well as to the University Y.M.C.A., where I served as counselor during the year.

David Belgum

TABLE
OF
CONTENTS

ix

GUILT:

Where Religion
And
Psychology Meet

INTRODUCTION:
PENANCE RECONSIDERED

By common consensus our sick society is in a value crisis. Moral relativism has led our people into confusion. Influential schools of psychology and sociology have convinced our generation that man, because of various types of determinism, is not genuinely responsible for his behavior.

According to the existentialists we are adrift on a sea of meaninglessness. Religious faith seems irrelevant to a "know-it-all" age of self-confident scientism. Supposedly, there is nothing that cannot be known or done if a large enough research grant for science and technology is made available to work on it. While, in the past, "hardness of heart" was considered an insurmountable obstacle to the healing of the soul, today it is assumed that science can force a "breakthrough" in the mental health problem. The Joint Commission on Mental

1

Illness and Health expects the solution to lie in adequate government expenditures for research and facilities. Man is adrift but too self-confident to use an anchor.

The behavioral sciences have promised a cure, if not for the value crisis, at least for the symptoms of mental illness. However, the cure offered by secular psychotherapy may be worse than the disease, as it strikes at what little moral guidance and theological anchorage is left. Not only is confidence in morality and conscience badly shaken, but the lack of scientific verification of significant results is disillusioning to the therapists themselves. What was once *sin* is now *sickness,* and, in spite of the quieting effects of tranquilizers, everyone agrees that the "disease" is spreading at an alarming rate.

Perhaps the most vocal, thoroughgoing, and controversial critic of contemporary psychotherapy and of religious practices is O. Hobart Mowrer.[1] It is ironic that such a stirring challenge to re-evaluate pastoral theology should come from the admittedly secular Psychology Department at the University of Illinois.

The churches can hardly be looked to as a rallying point because they have abdicated the mental health field and have repudiated or diluted many of their most effective methods. The social sheen of hypocrisy makes it difficult to deal forthrightly with sins in those established churches through which the "organization man" passes in his search for status and "upward mobility."

The more the churches fail to deal with, or feel themselves unqualified to cope with, particular sins, the more these problems are taken elsewhere—to Alcoholics Anonymous, mental health clinics, social service agencies, and mental hospitals.

---

[1] O. Hobart Mowrer, *The Crisis in Psychiatry and Religion* (Princeton, New Jersey: D. Van Nostrand Co., Inc., 1961).

The clergy, especially those who are leaders in pastoral theology and pastoral care, have attempted a dialogue with the behavioral sciences, but the "dialogue" has been one-sided, with the clergy listening, gullibly, to the current solution according to psychiatry, psychology, sociology, and anthropology.

The clergy will not have met the challenge of the dialogue successfully until it is as natural for psychotherapists and clinical psychologists to learn from and converse with a theological faculty, as it now is for the pastoral theologians and clergymen to do the reverse.

For the past sixteen years the writer has had the mistaken notion that if he could do good, competent, secular psychotherapy in a church building or while wearing a clerical collar, somehow it would come out as pastoral care. He has sensed that this notion is as unsatisfactory for many of his colleagues as it is for himself.

Looking backward through church history, we can see the rich variety of methods the church has tried in its pastoral care of souls. We should pause before we throw out a resource that has had great practical value and theological validity, but we should feel quite free also to experiment as boldly as did our predecessors.

What we need today is ecumenical conversation concerning the basic issues and tested practices of pastoral care. Laying aside all polemical adiaphora and furling any party flags designed to foster in-group loyalty, let us take a fresh look at the pastoral-care resources available to the churches. How can we incorporate these insights into an indigenous pastoral care? There may be something at the core of common theory and practice in our pastoral-care heritage which would be as valuable for ecumenicity as has been the revival of interdenominational interest in Biblical scholarship and worship.

Let us take a second look at the various forms that penance has taken in Christianity. Regardless of what it has been called, it has fulfilled certain common, essential, psychological functions in the cure of souls. And, theologically, its purpose has always been to take the sinner from the "Kingdom of Darkness" into the "Kingdom of Light."

The purpose of the mid-week prayer meeting was the *conversion* (*metanoia*) of the sinner. *Testimony* (confession) of the evil deeds for which the sinner desired help was heard, and *witnessing* to the new life in Christ and the "deeds worthy of repentance," often short lived, was encouraged. The Sacrament of Penance has three essential parts: *contrition* (again *metanoia*); *confession,* or admission of sins against God and neighbor; and *satisfaction,* or righteous and religious works to validate one's repentance. Often the "good works" of satisfaction among Roman Catholics are only of a token or symbolic nature and are emphasized as little as are "good works" among Lutherans.

Whether the means used is the "banning and shunning" of the Anabaptists, the church discipline of Calvin or Knox, Luther's form for confession and absolution, the "Method" John Wesley used with his bands and classes, or the penance of Eastern Orthodox, Anglican, or Roman Catholic traditions, the aim and purpose (and much of the psychological dynamics) of the churches are the same: to use effectively the "Keys of the Kingdom" to free the sinner from the fetters of sin, to heal the broken-hearted through the "ministry of reconciliation," and to restore the penitent to the righteous fellowship of the church.

The mentally ill might well ask if they are not the proper objects of the church's ministry, for one need not work long nor be very sophisticated in the field of mental illness to notice how often sin and guilt appear in case after case. Even some noted secular psychotherapists admit that the symptoms of the mentally ill are the amplified and distorted voice of conscience. Their "disease" is the price they pay for their alienation from their fellows and their disobedience to the moral demands of society.

Meanwhile, we must redirect our attention to the church's historic ministry to man's sin and guilt through penance, or its equivalent. Let us not bicker about terms but be sure that this particular aspect of the church's mission is being carried out with fullest efficacy. With contemporary society proclaiming that secular psychotherapy can deal better with sin and guilt than the churches, it is high time to ask, "Can the churches make the confessional functional?"

1

HYPOCRISY
AND MENTAL HEALTH

Beware of the leaven of the Pharisees,
which is hypocrisy. Nothing is covered
up that will not be revealed, or hidden
that will not be known. Whatever you
have said in the dark shall be heard in
the light, and what you have whispered
in private rooms shall be proclaimed
upon the housetops.[1]

Jesus reacted to sinners of many kinds—adulterers, thieves, and crooked tax collectors—with forgiveness and healing, but was hard toward the Pharisees because of their particular sin, hypocrisy.

In the twenty-third chapter of *Matthew,* Jesus is very severe, quite different from the gentle image we see elsewhere. He says to his disciples, "The scribes and the Pharisees sit on Moses' seat; so practice and observe whatever they tell you, but not what they do; for they preach, but do not practice." [2] Whereas to the woman taken in adultery he can say, "Neither

[1] *Luke* 12:1b-3.
[2] *Matthew* 23:2-3.

do I condemn you; go, and do not sin again."[3] Against the Pharisees he thunders, "Woe to you, scribes and Pharisees, hypocrites! for you are like whitewashed tombs, which outwardly appear beautiful, but within they are full of dead men's bones and all uncleanness. So you also outwardly appear righteous to men, but within you are full of hypocrisy and iniquity."[4]

Hypocrisy is such a serious matter because it is not like many other sins—stealing, murder, adultery, etc.; it is a *method* of dealing with sin which prevents a solution. In this sense it is the opposite of repentance and confession, and like other psychological defense mechanisms, it prevents one from facing reality objectively.

Hypocrisy and the "Split Personality"

One of the most devastating descriptions of a person is that he is "two-faced." Schizophrenia means, literally, "split mind" or, popularly, "split personality." A vast array of unsavory terms comes to mind to describe the behavior of the hypocrite: treachery, insincerity, lying, perjury, deceit, fraud, affectation, duplicity, undependability. Mentally, the most extreme form of dishonesty or duplicity is a schizophrenic break with reality in which John Jones believes he is Napoleon or John the Baptist. Regardless of the psychodynamics involved, it is unfortunately true that the schizophrenic turns a false face toward the outside world. Saint James said, "A double-minded man is unstable in all his ways."[5]

[3] *John* 8:11b.
[4] *Matthew* 23:27-28.
[5] *James* 1:8.

The Hebrew equivalent of hypocrisy in the Old Testament is *alam,* meaning to veil from sight or to conceal. Similar to Jesus' illustration comparing the Pharisees to a cup clean outside but dirty inside, are the following words from *Proverbs:*

> Like the glaze covering an earthen vessel
>   are smooth lips with an evil heart.
> He who hates, dissembles with his lips
>   and harbors deceit in his heart. . . .
> though his hatred be covered with guile,
>   his wickedness will be exposed in the assembly.[6]

Originally the Greek word, *hypokrisis,* meant to reply or answer; eventually it was employed as a term for the "reply" in Greek drama. The New Testament uses it in this sense—play acting or impersonating someone—pretending to be what in fact one is not.

The Romans used the same kind of word to describe man's characteristic way of representing himself. Personality or "person" is derived from two words, *per* and *sonare,* meaning to sound through, in this case to speak through a mask. An actor "pretended" he was happy by holding a laughing mask in front of his face while he spoke his lines. It was just as simple to be sad—by holding up the crying mask.

When we read in a theatre program before a play that an actor is going to pretend to be someone else on stage, it is not a sin, it is entertainment. However, when we think we can get by with pretense and sham in daily life, by pretending that the mask is our true image, it is hypocritical, sinful and dangerous.

An attractive and vivacious married woman who was

---

[6] *Proverbs* 26:23, 24, and 26.

active in her church, the local **P.T.A.**, many women's clubs, and was an advisor for a local 4-H Club was thought to be a model wife, mother, and civic servant. But behind her mask of respectability lay immoral acts and habits about which she did not want the community to know. She suffered a simulated, or psychosomatic, heart attack, and because she was unable to use her numerous activities as a defense, she sank into a deep psychotic depression and had to be committed to a state mental hospital. She began to recover when she gave up hypocrisy in favor of honesty, and when she brought her exterior image and her inner self into conformity. In short, she was no longer deliberately two-faced. She could admit who she really was, and she began to be the kind of person the community believed her to be. Although it was not an easy task to change a long, deeply rooted pattern of duplicity, she became increasingly integrated and able to live effectively. It was as though she were echoing the words of the Psalmist: "Vindicate me, O Lord, for I have walked in my integrity."[7]

Hypocrisy is as disastrous to us personally as it is to our country when someone pretends to be a friend, but is actually an enemy—and treason is the most heinous of crimes. No wonder Jesus warned people against hypocrisy, for he could help only those who would admit who they really were and the fact that something was wrong in their lives. Those who say they are healthy will not send for a physician. We use hypocrisy to try to hide a part or all of ourselves because we are ashamed of being known. We feel guilt but do not want to face the consequences, so we pretend all is well. If a person is afraid to be known for what he is, he feels guilty and alienated from God, as well as from his community. *Genesis* records the classic story of such hiding:

[7] *Psalm* 26:1.

And they heard the sound of the Lord God walking in the cool of the day, and the man and his wife hid themselves from the presence of the Lord God among the trees of the garden. But the Lord God called to the man, and said to him, "Where are you?" And he said, "I heard the sound of thee in the garden, and I was afraid, because I was naked; and I hid myself." He said, "Who told you that you were naked? Have you eaten of the tree of which I commanded you not to eat?"[8]

Hiding and hypocrisy did not work for Adam, it did not work for the Pharisees, and it won't work for us today.

The Futility of Hypocrisy

Jesus said very simply, "Nothing is covered up that will not be revealed, or hidden that will not be known."

In the writer's capacity as counselor to seminary students, he was oversolicitous in assuring them that all information from the psychological tests would be kept confidential. He still plans to preserve this confidence, but he will also assure them that if there is a quirk in their personality, it is probably no secret anyway. It is pointless for a student who argues vociferously with his professors, his classmates, and his roommates, and who has lost a couple of girl friends a year because of his sarcasm, to hope that the psychological test administrator or counselor will not discover that he has an aggressive or hostile streak in his personality. People already know it and worry about him. They wish they could help, but he is beyond help at present because he is pretending not to have

[8] *Genesis* 3:8-11.

any problems. How often we try to keep our sins secret. We pretend to the community and even to those closest to us that all is well, but we fool no one.

A man who is having an affair with his secretary may think his alibis are perfect, but soon his children begin to ask, "Why is Daddy so different lately?" The mother cannot give a good answer, but she has thought of many things. One wife even checked with the company auditor, thinking the husband was suffering from financial worries. He had become edgy, sometimes depressed, usually anxious, but no one could help him because he would not let them know who he really was. He was pretending to be someone else, and it was soul-destroying and marriage-destroying. It was the opposite of openness and repentance; it was the opposite of ". . . putting away falsehood, let every one speak truth with his neighbor for we are members one of another." [9]

It is strange that this man should delude himself into feeling quite "safe" in this hypocritical situation, for, almost inevitably, his world will crumble. Who knows when his secret will be revealed—through a rumor, a stomach ulcer, a psychotic depression, or in some other manner. "Nothing is covered up that will not be revealed."

Nor is the man who drinks too much going to tell anybody. He is going to keep it a secret as long as possible. One restored alcoholic told an Alcoholics Anonymous meeting how he used to hide liquor under the various parts of his printing press, and was still finding half empty half-pints when he repaired or maintained his machinery. One of the great joys of his present life is that he is not continually *hiding* parts of his life from his wife, customers, or friends.

Nor is the person who eats too much going to share what-

[9] *Ephesians* 4:25.

ever anxiety it is that drives her to find food as a substitute for life. Nor will the polite chiseler on income tax usually tell anyone how he managed to sneak by without paying his share, that is, unless he has the character disorder of a morally undeveloped psychopath. Nor the one who hates his father—and the list grows ad infinitum.

How Hypocrisy Thwarts
the Church's Ministry of Healing

Let us suppose that a thousand people in a church pretend to be completely free from sin. Twenty of them are alcoholics; but none will believe that he can find help in the church since the other nine hundred ninety-nine members are all "saints" who have never been defeated by sin or tempted as they have been. These twenty alcoholics will have to go to Alcoholics Anonymous since *there* are fellow sinners who have overcome this tragedy in their lives. The writer says, "Thank God for Alcoholics Anonymous," but he also has an uneasy feeling that it is an indictment against the church and that hypocrisy prevented the church from performing its duty. As has so often happened, when the church has failed in some aspect of its mission, other agencies have arisen to fill the void.

The fifty members of our hypothetical church who have committed adultery, or whose marriages are falling apart, will have to go to "divorcees anonymous," marriage counselors, and/or social service agencies. None of them can believe that any of the other nine hundred ninety-nine "nice" members of their church have had serious problems, or that they could receive the understanding, forgiveness, healing, and social encouragement needed for a new life within the church fellowship.

The one hundred "members" (but surely not "members one of another," as cited in *Ephesians* above) who suffer from neurotic anxiety, psychotic depression, or thoughts of suicide, and/or sufficient maladjustment to rely regularly on any of a dozen tranquilizers on the market, will have to seek out mental health clinics and psychiatrists, because they will believe that no one else of the thousand in the "household of faith" has ever been so afflicted. For as they look about them they see only "good" people who could not possibly share their problems, temptations, sins, and defeats. They evidently do not believe the Scripture verse they heard read in the worship service, "For there is no distinction; since all have sinned and fall short of the glory of God." [10]

Hypocrisy thwarts the healing of the church in two ways. First, it is impossible to help another when one is blinded by hypocrisy—Jesus asked, "Can a blind man lead a blind man? Will they not both fall into a pit?"[11] Secondly, it is impossible to be helped. One turns for help to those genuine and honest persons who have come through great tragedy themselves or who, for some other reason know "the way" that leads to abundant life.

The plea for privileged communication and the secrecy of private confession is due to the rejection, which to the sinner seems inevitable, were the congregation to know his true nature.

In the early church we have a beautiful example of the great struggle of the penitent against the powers of darkness,

[10] *Romans* 3:23.
[11] *Luke* 6:39b.

with the members of the congregation as witnesses and sup-
porters in the fight against sin and despair:

> The rite of *exomologesis* . . . is an act of self-humiliation
> by the penitent, calculated to win the compassion of the
> congregation. The penitent already sleeps in sackcloth,
> dresses in rags, feeds little and austerely, and spends long
> hours in deprecatory prayer. To encourage him, Tertullian
> has said that God leaves the gate of forgiveness ajar, so that
> the Christian sinner can find the means of obtaining forgive-
> ness, Second Repentance, in the vestibule. This figure of
> speech seems to hint at the actual rite of *exomologesis,* for
> the vestibule of the house of liturgical gathering is the place
> where the penitent makes public his need of penance. As the
> brethren arrive for the liturgy, he prostrates himself at the
> feet of the presbyters, kneels to "confessors" (those who have
> steadfastly borne persecution) and begs the intercession of all
> who enter.[12]

In despair the sinner struggles in solitude. The odds seem
overwhelmingly against him. But supported and encouraged
by other rescued believers, he takes hope in the possibility
that victory can be his also. Latourette describes the scene of
battle:

> If the sin had been publicly known, restoration must also be
> made in public. In the churches in the West, especially in
> Rome, a place was appointed in which penitents stood and
> mourned until the completion of the service. They then cast
> themselves prostrate on the ground with groans and lamenta-
> tions. The bishop, weeping, also cast himself on the ground,
> and the congregation wept and groaned. The bishop then

[12] W. Telfer, *The Forgiveness of Sins* (Philadelphia: Muhlenberg Press, 1960), pp. 48-49.

arose, offered a prayer for the penitents, and dismissed them.[13]

Imagine the contrast between the situation where the sinner knows he has Christ, the Communion of Saints, and his loved ones in the local congregation fighting with him against Satan, and, on the other hand, when the sinner seems by every indication to be standing not only against the Devil and the dark powers of this world, but *also* against the congregation. In his solitary fear and overwhelming isolation, he does not speak out in repentance and confession, but practices hypocrisy. And, of course, he is not healed.

What would be the nature of a hypothetical church in which the thousand members believed that they had, individually, as the Scripture says, "sinned and fall[en] short of the glory of God"? They would each be ready to join in the battle against sin, to aid their fallen brother in the resolution of his guilt, and to support him in victorious living; and there would be a very good chance for victory. Would they not feel free to "Bear one another's burdens, and so fulfill the law of Christ" [14] out of gratitude for their own victories over their own sins and weaknesses? If each of the thousand, instead of practicing hypocrisy, had dealt with his or her own infirmity honestly and openly, it would be quite natural to follow Christ's admonition in the Sermon on the Mount:

Judge not, that you be not judged. For with the judgment you pronounce you will be judged, and the measure you give

[13] Kenneth Scott Latourette, *A History of Christianity* (New York: Harper and Row, Publishers, 1953), p. 217.
[14] *Galatians* 6:2.

will be the measure you get. Why do you see the speck that is
in your brother's eye, but do not notice the log that is in
your own eye? . . . You hypocrite, first take the log out of
your own eye, and then you will see clearly to take the speck
out of your brother's eye.[15]

The implications that hypocrisy and its opposite, confession, have for mental health will be further explored in later
chapters. There are theological, sociological, and psychological ramifications, as well as practical applications, involved in
this issue. The church has a divine antidote for the soul-
sickness of hypocrisy if its resources can be made available to
those whose only solution to sin has been disastrous duplicity.

[15] *Matthew* 7:1-3, 5.

2

THE TRIAD
OF MORALITY

The three learned professions and the three "superior faculties" of the fully developed medieval university were theology, law, and medicine. Any and all of these rested on the broad base of the liberal arts such as logic, rhetoric, arithmetic, and music. When concerned with the deeper, the basic issues of life, the three classic categories predominated, among which theology stood out as "The Queen of the Sciences."

Law dealt with the necessary social fabric of interpersonal relationships. In this sense the medieval faculty of law might be considered an ancestor of modern sociology and social work as well as of law as we know it. Medicine was the study of the personal or intra-personal self. If there had been modern psychological study in the Middle Ages, it probably would have come under this discipline. It dealt with man's individual welfare in contrast to his social welfare. Theology was the over-arching perspective that gave both law and medicine meaning and coherence. Therefore, no matter what sphere of life was being considered, the personal or the inter-personal, it was finally viewed from a theological perspective, and seen in a cosmic dimension.

In analyzing the nature and solution of personal guilt, it is useful to apply the three classic disciplines of theology, law, and medicine as a triad of morality. We may set the three side by side as we describe (1) the categories of morality, (2) the problem of sin and guilt, and (3) the solution to the problem of sin and guilt. (See Tables 1, 2, and 3.)

Table 1

THE CATEGORIES OF MORALITY

Discipline	*Theology*	*Law*	*Medicine*
Dimension	Cosmic	Social	Personal
Subject	Creator	Ecclesia	Imago Dei
Ethical obligation	Love God	Love neighbor	Love self

The basic assumption of the Christian view of the universe today, as well as in medieval times, is that there exists a Reality beyond the individual self and even beyond the collection of selves called society. In fact the universe of physical nature itself cannot be fully accounted for by adding up the sum total of all its parts. There is beyond all things and all persons the Creator of all things and all persons, God. Philosophically, this approach may be called supernaturalism and is in a sense the cornerstone of religion as such. Various terms come to mind: the "Wholly Other," "First Cause,"

"Ultimate Reality," etc., but most commonly in Christianity, "God the Creator." Some refer to this as a vertical relationship or axis.

There is also the social relationship or horizontal axis, for man is born into society. It is assumed that man does not, perhaps cannot, have a moral relationship with God in isolation; he is not so constructed. Hence, we have from earliest Old Testament times the concept of the individual as an integral part of the community, "the Chosen People," "the People of Israel," "the Children of Abraham," a covenantal relationship. In the New Testament there is the "Ecclesia," those who have been "called out" of the world into a communing fellowship with God.

Unfortunately there has often been posed an unnecessary cleavage between these two relationships as though man's moral choice was an either/or dilemma. But the choice is not that man must relate *either* to God his Creator *or* to his fellowman; it is rather an inseparable "both/and" situation. The illustration of vertical and horizontal lines intersecting at the individual thus: $\uparrow$ GOD $\leftarrow$FELLOW MAN$\rightarrow$ is an over-simplification. Perhaps there should be a three-dimensional or conical diagram to portray the social context within which God relates to man and from within which man responds to God. Jesus said that inasmuch as anyone showed love to one of the least of his brethren he was showing that love also toward Jesus himself. Christian morality allows for no dichotomy here but proceeds one step further.

The individual also has a value in and of himself, as a person. He derives his worth from the fact that he was created in the Image of God and endowed with the capacity to achieve a self-conscious personality. The nature and destiny of man are seen in eternal perspective. He is not only born into a community, but has the capacity for communion or fellowship with his Creator *and* with his fellowmen.

Just as there are three dimensions: cosmic, social, and personal; so there are three subjects involved: God the Creator, the individual person created by God, and the social community in which he exists. And in each of these dimensions, or with each of these persons, there is inherent a necessary ethical obligation. Jesus summed it up in answer to the question about which is the greatest commandment. He said, as in one breath, that man must love God, his neighbor, and himself. Here too there is no either/or alternative for man. All three ethical obligations are interdependent and inseparable.

One cannot separate himself from God without doing violence to the Image of God (*Imago Dei*) woven into the fabric of his own nature; nor can one violate his ethical relationships and obligations to his neighbor or larger society without doing damage and violence to himself; nor can one do violence to himself or his neighbor without offending God the Creator, or without interfering with God's providential care of the man himself and his neighbor.

Before proceeding to a discussion of the problem of sin and guilt, it is necessary to see this total picture of the interdependent categories of morality. A partial perspective leads to inadequate understanding of the problem and an oversimplification of the solution. Examples of partial perspectives have been: (1) the Hedonism which asks simply "What is good for *me;* what makes *me* feel good?"; (2) the Nazi in-group thinking that asks "What is good for *our* group, *our* country, *our* race?"; and (3) the supposedly spiritualized and other-worldly view which says simply, "It doesn't matter what happens to me or my neighbor as long as *I'm right with God.*"

We turn next to the problem of sin and guilt, and the breakdown in morality. Table 2 provides a schematic outline for this analysis.

Table 2

THE PROBLEM OF SIN AND GUILT

Discipline	Theology	Law	Medicine
Nature of sin	Aversion from God	Voluntary act	Causes defect of character
Grave sins	Apostasy	Murder	Concupiscence
Consequences of sins	Penitent	Prisoner	Patient (personal maladjustment)

The nature of sin may be described under the three disciplines of theology, law and medicine; or to put it in terms of relationships, as affecting man's relationship with God, with his neighbor, and with himself. Sin in its initial inception is a turning away from or an aversion from God. Another characteristic necessary to make a deed, word, thought, or condition a sin is *responsibility.* Classically, volition is essential to sin. Was it a voluntary act, one for which the person can legitimately be held responsible? Law is much concerned with this question: "To what extent was the person responsible for this crime?" This not only helps to determine guilt but also the extent or intensity of the punishment inflicted by society. Finally, the nature of sin may be seen in the interior condition of the sinner. A defect of character is involved. Just as in the ethical obligation to love self, sin cannot exist or operate only in relationship to God and neighbor, it also affects the self, the character.

There have been many lists of sins, and they can be classified in various ways, but the three grave or capital sins of apostolic and post-apostolic times were apostasy, murder, and concupiscence. In the Sermon on the Mount Jesus singles out certain commandments for interpretation; killing (*Matthew* 5:21), adultery (*Matthew* 5:27), and the danger of idolatry or diluted worship (*Matthew* 5:33). Concerning the early church, McNeill writes: "There was much hesitation even about admitting to repentance and reconciliation those who had committed the grave sins of idolatry, unchastity, and the shedding of blood."[1] The catalog of "works of the flesh" listed in *Galatians* 5:19b-20 appear to fall under these three headings, although they surely overlap:

Apostasy	*Murder*	*Concupiscence*
Sins vs. God	*Sins vs. Neighbor*	*Sins vs. Self*
idolatry	enmity	immorality, impurity
sorcery	strife	licentiousness
	party spirit	envy, anger
	dissensions	selfishness
		drunkenness
		carousing

In our day, as in Paul's, more attention is paid to the great variety of sins in the individual's personality which are obvious and external, but the shorter list under "apostasy" must not be misleading. The sin of unbelief is all pervasive and desperately serious. Alienation from God is disastrous even when it may not be as obvious externally as drunkenness or murder. But again we must emphasize the interrelatedness

---

[1] John T. McNeill, *A History of the Cure of Souls* (New York: Harper & Row, Publishers, 1951), p. 89.

of these sins, for man's sin in one sphere of relationships is bound to affect his relationships in the other two.

The most obvious consequence of sin and crime is the punishment inflicted by the laws of society. The *prisoner* is deprived of the rights and privileges of citizenship in his society. Punishment is terminated when the demands of society have been met, when the penalty has been paid. Then he can be restored to fellowship with his neighbor. But usually we think of the prisoner as one who is apprehended by force and "brought to justice." He is an unwilling pupil and the lesson of morality is forced upon him. Yet, during the course of his imprisonment or even during his trial he may shift to another approach, that of the penitent.

The *penitent* takes the religious stance. A consequence of his sin is that he senses his alienation from God and neighbor; and he desires to be restored to fellowship again. Under the theological perspective he becomes acutely aware of his unworthiness and guilt. He has been a poor and irresponsible steward of the gifts which God has entrusted to him. He has violated a sacred trust by the misuse of nature, by the squandering of his personal resources, or self, or has withdrawn from community into anti-social egotism. But whatever his sin, he sees it as guilt before God, and it makes him penitent.

Karen Horney[2] speaks of distressed persons moving in various directions: moving against, moving toward, moving away from. We may say that the criminal is moving against society in open rebellion and belligerent aggression. The penitent is moving toward society in the sense that he is seeking to be restored to community, to fellowship, and to relationship with God and neighbor. The third alternative is the

[2] Karen Horney, *Our Inner Conflicts* (New York: W. W. Norton & Company, 1945).

least realistic—moving away from society. This is retreat and withdrawal into a seemingly less threatening but increasingly isolated world. This is the fantasy world of mental illness.

The *patient* may suffer in many ways as a result of sin (see Chapter 4, "Patient or Penitent"). For our purposes in analyzing the consequences of sin we note that this reaction falls under the discipline of medicine and deals with the personal and psychic welfare of the individual. It is also closely related to the "defect of character" described under "nature of sin." The suffering may continue to afflict him even though the legal arm of society never punishes him. The term "patient" is used in the schematic outline rather than the narrower label "psychotic" since a great variety of physical and mental maladies may result from sin.

But more important than classification and analysis of the problems of morality is the healing of the breakdown, the solution to the problem of sin and guilt.

Table 3

THE SOLUTION OF THE PROBLEM OF SIN AND GUILT

Discipline	Theology	Law	Medicine
Virtues	Faith	Hope	Love
Penance	Contrition	Confession	Satisfaction
Result	Salvation	Communion	Vocation

It is not surprising that historic Christianity should propose the three theological virtues of faith, hope, and love, to counterbalance the three grave or capital sins of apostasy, murder, and concupiscence. These negative poisons require strong positive antidotes. The sinner has frequently lost a sense of meaning in his life as he has cut himself off from God. Meaninglessness is closely related to unbelief. In his relationships with others he is often in despair and feels hopeless. He doubts that restoration to community is possible in his case because his aggression and hostilities have pushed others farther and farther away from him, till it seems impossible to bridge the chasm between himself and his neighbor. And as for love of self, this is completely missing if he is at all aware of his sin. He senses himself to be unworthy and unable to make any contribution to society—he is "good for nothing." The psychopathic deviate may not sense this estrangement, but his defect is due to such a grievous lack of socialization that he feels no guilt and does not recognize right from wrong, sin from virtue.

Before we discuss the cure peculiar to the Christian church, namely: The Office of the Keys, or penance, it will be necessary to consider the concept of forgiveness. Interestingly enough, forgiveness is not listed as one of the "parts" of penance because it is not a step or process performed by the sinner, nor is it an end in itself. It is provided by others, by God and neighbor. It is a condition and it is a means. If forgiveness is symbolized at all in the Office of the Keys, it would be the turning of the key in the lock. But the sole purpose of turning a key in a lock is to unlock the door and enable one to go into the next room, i.e. to pass out of bondage into freedom. It is not enough to be stuck or fixated in a key-turning syndrome. The goal is not forgiveness, but the restored fellowship with God and neighbor and self for which forgiveness paves the way. And fellowship involves the willingness of both parties.

Telfer describes forgiveness in a functional manner:

. . . In that field (of human social relations), the natural reaction of a person sinned against is to retaliate. In life lived at an animal level, retaliation for offense is automatic and inevitable. But human culture gives rise to considerations which restrain or modify such reaction. The desire for retaliation may depart altogether, if the offender shows that his offense was not intentional; for it is at least as much the intention as the behavior, which constitutes the sin where civilized men and women are concerned. Even where the sin was, at the time, deliberate, the same result may follow, if the offender, afterwards, comes to a different mind and shows sincere concern to make amends. As the sin took place in time past, he cannot undo it. But he can so desire to dissociate himself from his sin as to prevail upon the offended person to restore their mutual relations to cordiality. Yielding to this generous impulse, he will think no more of retaliation. And it is this act of generosity that bears the name of forgiveness.

The English word "forgive" (like French *pardonner* and German *vergeben*) is simply a strengthened form of the verb to give or grant. And the reason for adopting this strengthened word-form is to emphasize the unconditional nature of the act which it represents. Now if the waiving of retaliation is to be unconditional, it must spring from kindness and good will on the part of the person who forgives. For if a person were to renounce retaliation because he feared the offender, or because he hoped, by so doing, to gain some future benefit by means of him, it would be no sign of good will. Furthermore, such renunciation would not be unconditional, and so could not rightly be called forgiveness.[3]

[3] W. Telfer, *The Forgiveness of Sins* (Philadelphia: Muhlenberg Press, 1960), pp. 8, 9. See also Hans Selye's *The Stress of Life* (New York: McGraw-Hill Book Company, Inc., 1956), for the suggestion that the opposite of retaliation is or ought to be *gratitude,* which interestingly comes from the same root as *grace.* Positive grace must supplant the negative and destructive power of sin. Theologically it is maintained that one does not generate this all by himself, but it must be mediated to him through the "ecclesia" from God. Such grace can be appropriated only when the sinner turns in faith and receptive dependence outward toward God and those in the ecclesia or church who will bring the Gospel or "Good News" of reconciliation to him.

Forgiveness, instead of being an end or goal in itself, is rather the very prerequisite, or atmosphere without which the whole process of reconciliation could not take place. Forgiveness is the hope that the sinner can again enter into relationship with God and neighbor instead of continuing as the hopeless victim of retaliation or alienation.

Traditionally, penance is said to consist of three parts: *contrition* or repentance, *confession,* and *satisfaction.*[4] The church has maintained that there is no short-cut, and although various traditions and denominations have emphasized different parts or used different terms, forgiveness and restoration to fellowship are dependent upon the three processes indicated above. They are the responsibility of the sinner.

Repentance or contrition, genuine sorrow for having offended another person, is an essential starting point on the road to recovery of community and interpersonal relationships. The opposite in Scripture is "hardness of heart," as when Pharaoh hardened his heart and would not let the Children of Israel go; instead, he continued unrepentant in the sin of enslavement, against God's will. But when King David saw the enormity of his sin against Uriah and Bathsheba, he was struck down with remorse and humbled himself before God's Altar and before the people of his kingdom.

A couple came to a counselor with a deep and involved marital problem which had degenerated for over fifteen years until it finally ended in infidelity. They were both highly intelligent and educated. They knew all the jargon of psychology and marriage counselors' manuals. But after about

---

[4] See the Bibliography for works dealing with the theology, history, and practice of penance and confession.

seven weeks of "trying everything," the therapy was terminated because neither one had yet reached "step one." Each
desired the reform of the other, but neither one felt genuine
remorse about his or her own shortcomings, failures, or sins.
This may not be too surprising since each held divorce as a
very real option. Neither one sensed the deep wounds that
were being inflicted upon the children. Neither was aware of
the enormity of his sin. Rather they looked upon the whole
affair as troublesome and uncomfortable. They wanted to be
rid of the symptom of their marital distress because it was
a nuisance. When the counseling was terminated they had
still not come to the point where they wished to make the
great sacrifice of remorse and repentance. It would have been
too humiliating; it was too much work.

Alcoholics often present the same pattern. For years they
begrudge the "morning after" hangover, the headaches, the
nuisance of having to pay for dented fenders and broken
furniture; the results of their drinking bouts. But true healing and restoration does not come until they want to be rid of
the sin more desperately than they wish to be rid of the
vexatious symptoms. One morning the drunkard wakes up in
a hospital, almost dead from pneumonia or shaking with
"D. T.'s," and he finds himself with a ninety-day workhouse
sentence; or he comes home to a house from which wife and
children have fled in disgust or fear. Whatever the reason that
prompts his sudden awakening, he is on the road to restoration when he sees himself as a sinner, as a man on the brink
of disaster, as a man who is *lost* in the full unutterable despair
of that term.

Sadly enough, psychotherapy, counseling, treatment of any
kind, is but marking time until the "client" takes step one,

repentance for sin, contrition and remorse concerning his broken relationships.

Confession is the opposite of hypocrisy (as discussed in Chapter 1). Confession consists of sharing with God and a symbolic representative of the community (and a varying number of others, depending upon the case and how these others might be involved) the nature and significance of his sins, without suspension of ethical responsibility.

In many ways the dynamics of confession are similar to the process in psychotherapy known as "catharsis." Catharsis (literally "cleansing"), likewise, involves the expression of negative feelings and past mistakes, but for which a sense of blame may or may not be present. In fact, in some forms of group therapy violent verbal blasts and expressions of hostility are encouraged and approved. The mere uninhibited release of libidinal energy is assumed to be therapeutic.

Confession, on the other hand, is highly structured. (See Chapter 5 for sample methods—from the traditions of seven denominations—for dealing with the problem of sin and guilt.) Judgment is not suspended since both penitent and confessor stand under the judgment of God, the Ten Commandments, and the voice of conscience. Guilt and responsibility are neither dodged nor shrugged off, but are accepted as realities. Such phrases as *"mea culpa"* or "it is my most grievous fault" may be used.

A young woman described her dealings with a clergyman who had followed this approach in the following words:

When I got kicked out of nursing school, my folks were upset, and my doctor said I needed help. He suggested I go to this minister for counseling. I guess I thought he'd explain

> what made me get into trouble like that and help me under-
> stand myself so it wouldn't happen again. But he wouldn't
> let me hedge on the problem, and finally I told him all about
> it (promiscuity). It was awfully painful and hard, but I guess
> it was best to get it all out in the open.

For the first time in her life she began to see that she had to
accept responsibility for her own life, her own behavior. Her
sophistication melted into sorrowful contrition. After thorough confession and restoration in the church, she accepted
responsibility for other areas of her life as well, and values
and religious concepts which had hitherto remained almost
meaningless to her became vital and functional.

In confession the person is accepted not in lieu of judgment but because grace and forgiveness make it possible to
accept the penitent in spite of judgment—as Shakespeare
said, "Mercy seasons justice." Love and mercy intervene to
rescue the sinner where justice might demand the pound of
flesh or complete destruction. A discussion of the doctrine of
the atonement is beyond the scope of this study, but the
rationale for the forgiveness and the absolution which follow
confession is to be found in the Second Article of the Apostles' Creed. Regardless of the various theories of the atonement, forgiveness is considered possible "for Christ's sake."

So far, in the solution to the problem of sin and guilt,
there is general agreement among the churches that repentance (contrition) and confession of sins are necessary for
forgiveness and full restoration to God and community. The
third step is controversial and subject to polemical distortion.

Satisfaction in Roman Catholic penance is sometimes misunderstood by Protestants to be a man-made substitute for the
Atonement of Christ. We need to dig beneath the theological

warfare of the sixteenth century to discover the dynamic function that is here alluded to. A casual perusal of Chapter 5 will clearly reveal that all seven denominations assume that the Christian restoration of the sinner does not stop with repentance, confession, and the absolution of forgiveness. The Third Article of the Apostles' Creed speaks about the work of the Holy Spirit, which among other things, is to promote sanctification, "growth in grace," the "new life in Christ." Just as we found a catalog of the "works of the flesh" (see page 22) in the *Epistle to the Galatians,* so we find a list of the "fruit of the Spirit" (5:22-23): "love, joy, peace, patience, kindness, goodness, faithfulness, gentleness, self-control."

One Protestant liturgical form of absolution adds, "and may the Lord grant you time for *amendment* of life." Surely, here is the exception that a more *satisfactory* life will follow the spiritual experience of repentance, confession, and forgiveness. The penitent is restored, but restored to what? To sin again? God forbid! Now the "good tree will bear good fruit" just as surely as the bad tree formerly bore bad fruit. The "fruit of the Spirit" is the evidence of the victorious life "in Christ" (as St. Paul calls it) as contrasted to the sinful life under the enslavement to the "Old Adam."

Here again an unfortunate and artificial "either/or" was posed in the heat of theological battle during the Reformation, so that many supposed they had to choose between *faith* and *good works* in their restoration. Two Scripture passages have often been quoted out of context and in opposition to each other—"The just shall live by faith" and "Faith without works is dead."

When both Jesus and St. Paul disparaged the "good works" of the Pharisees and scribes, we must remember that these *hypocrites* were not doing truly good works, either *be-*

fore or *after* forgiveness; in fact, in their self-righteousness they felt no need for forgiveness, for they never suspected themselves of sinning. Their very hypocrisy was exemplified by the pretense of external show of religious righteousness "tithing mint, and anise, and cummin," praying in public, counting the number of tassels on their liturgically "correct" garments, etc. Jesus called this the clean outside of the cup or the whited outside of the sepulchre. Their inner life, in terms of concern for the needs of their suffering brethren, was a dark contrast, for in actual practice they "passed by on the other side," did not care for widows and orphans, and, as Jesus said, neglected the weightier matters of the Law: love, mercy, justice, etc. They had an intellectual "belief" in the Shema and Jehovah, but that is neither what Paul nor James meant by "faith." Faith is the all-pervasive power that enters a life and transforms all one's relationships.

Rather than to quibble about the details and terms of the forgiven, transformed, restored life of the penitent, can we not all agree that this function must be present or the penitent has not been brought all the way back to fellowship with God, his neighbor, or himself? (Constructive proposals concerning these problems will be presented in Chapter 7, "A Functional Confessional.")

What is the end *result* for persons who have had the problem of sin and guilt solved according to the above therapy of penance?

Salvation is the traditional theological term implying restoration to God within the eternal perspective. It is a cosmic healing that goes beyond getting rid of bothersome symptoms, that goes beyond a mere time and space solution. It means a person is restored both here and hereafter; it is total.

Communion with one's neighbor is again possible with nothing to hide and no bitterness or retaliation to fear. Those who used to feel safe in hypocrisy and duplicity discover that confession opens up new channels of communication that they had never dreamed possible, with loved ones and strangers alike. Gone are the rationalizations, the lying; many defense mechanisms can now be discarded. The love of neighbor is now possible.

A sense of *vocation* can be restored, or perhaps, truly sensed for the first time. The penitent has discovered his true worth as a "child of God" and as his "brother's keeper." He is needed in the world to foster God's providence for some segment of the world (be it a hay field or a machine shop) or of society (be it as social worker or laundress). He now sees and can love himself appropriately, realistically.

The result of the solution to the problem of sin and guilt is that he is free (yet of course still in a finite way) to love God and his neighbor as himself.

3

A DILEMMA
OF THE PSYCHOTHERAPIST

Turning from the medieval Christian triad of morality to the modern view of man and his problems, we find the threefold pattern still useful for analysis. For though the twentieth century American intelligentsia may reject the term "theology" and even deny its admission into most public universities, systems of belief, even when not explicitly admitted, still operate to provide basic assumptions and a rationale for personal and social behavior. Theology may no longer be referred to as the Queen of the Sciences, and the nature of law and medicine may have changed greatly, but the old problems of sin and guilt, the questions of morality and ethical behavior, the breakdown and restoration of relationships continue to plague us.

Psychotherapy has become increasingly *the* hope of those with problems and various kinds of "breakdown" in personal and social adjustment. Even though this new "salvation" is based on scientific principles and would generally deny having a *theology,* we shall use the three categories mentioned in the previous chapter to indicate the cosmic, social, and personal dimensions of the problems of sin and guilt and their resolution. This approach makes comparison with the previous chapter easier.

Another introductory note is necessary before we begin the discussion of the psychotherapist's dilemma. It is unfair for the church to put all the blame on the psychotherapist for secularizing the problem of sin and guilt as well as its solution. In many ways theology and the church abdicated the field. Chapters 5 and 6 indicate how far the contemporary churches have wandered from their initial charge to deal squarely with the problems of sin and guilt. Movements such as rationalism, certain kinds of liberalism, and the anti-historical impact of democratic conformity helped to weaken the church's ministry in this regard. And whenever one insti-

Table 4

SECULAR PSYCHOTHERAPY'S APPROACH TO THE MORAL PROBLEM

Discipline (Dimension)	*Theology* (Cosmic)	*Law* (Social)	*Medicine* (Personal)
Philosophy	Naturalism	Determinism	Materialism
Ethics	Moral Relativism	Individualism	Hedonism
Consequence of the Problem	Meaninglessness	Irresponsi- bility	Illness
Solution of the Problem	Scientific Objectivity	Permissive- ness	Catharsis and Insight

tution vacates its responsibility, others rush in to fill the vacuum. Now, if a man commits adultery, embezzles money from his company, or does other immoral acts, the clergy-man, as well as the judge, recommends psychotherapy. Per-haps medicine is becoming the queen of the three professions, with law and theology being subsumed under its science. While we may be grateful for the sincere efforts of secular psychotherapists, we can be of most help by trying to under-stand the problems they face in *their* approach to sin and guilt.

Naturalism is the philosophical stance of most psycho-therapists and psychologists. One eminent psychologist at a large university stated that he doubted if more than a hand-ful of the seventy colleagues in his department were super-naturalists. Many who have undergone an intensive period of experimental and clinical psychology have ceased to state their philosophy positively and merely say they are uninter-ested in "metaphysical" questions or "just don't know." Others are as dogmatic about their creed of naturalism as is the most fervent Bible-belt evangelist. Some, if pressed, would claim to be logical positivists.

The educational route to psychotherapist-status is thor-oughly scientific, whether it be via experimental and clinical psychology or medical school. The empirical method, the statistical approach, and experimental controls supposedly yield valid and reliable knowledge. The field of investigation is limited to observable data and "testable hypotheses." Since religious concepts and experiences seem not to lend them-selves to such investigation, they are often relegated to the realm of irrelevant superstition and magic. The orientation becomes "secular" in significant ways. Without the cosmic dimension it is hard to account for all the facts; this becomes clear under the next (social) dimension of this philosophy.

Determinism is a natural corollary of naturalistic philosophy. Within this limited universe man is presumed to live in a closed system of observable mechanistic events. Since all that exists must ultimately be knowable by finite man, society must be scaled down to be encompassed by man's five senses, preferably in the laboratory or under controlled experimental conditions. Although behaviorism is perhaps the most extreme form of determinism, with its stimulus = response (S = R) explanation for man's actions, the question, "What *made* him do it?" is common among many who would not call themselves behaviorists or reflexologists.

Gordon W. Allport has long been a champion against this reductionist tendency, as has the existentialist Viktor Frankl. If such voices are heeded, it will help the psychotherapist out of the dilemma of trying to make too little philosophy do too much. Allport's criticism is to the point:

> Strict determinism would have to say that no one ever *does* anything. The person does not live his life; it is lived for him. He is no freer than a billiard ball responding within a triangle of forces. The two major forces are internal drives and environmental pressure. To these two Freud added a third, namely, man's super-ego. This force, however, is only a derivative of parental and social teaching (environmental forces). The ego, having no energy of its own, is a victim of these tyrants. . . .
>
> All these pressures exist. But *becoming* is the process by which all these forces are employed by the creative urge to program a style of life for oneself. The basic existentialist urge to grow, pursue meaning, seek unity is also a "given." It is a major fact even more prominent in man's nature than his propensity to yield to surrounding pressures. It is this desire for autonomy, for individuation, for selfhood, for

existential uniqueness that enters into the shaping of the product. Growth toward this end is a law to which most personalities seem to conform.[1]

In the previous chapter we stated that one aspect of the nature of sin is its voluntary character. A person can thus be held responsible by his fellowmen. It would put a therapist in a serious dilemma to hold to a behavioristic theory of determinism and at the same time hold a client responsible to any serious degree for his own problem, his own sins against his fellowmen or against his own nature. In fact the terms "sin" and "responsibility" are left out of the terminology of a large number of secular psychotherapists. It becomes difficult to speak of a *moral* problem or of *responsibility* to society.

Materialism becomes man's personal philosophy according to the naturalistic view of the universe. Since there is no Person behind the world of things, even other persons become things, objects instead of subjects. As Allport says, characterizing this positivist view of man, "Man is like inanimate objects (including machines) and like elementary organisms."[2] Surely this lowers his own self-concept, self-esteem, and notion of where he belongs in the scheme of things. Surely it makes a difference in one's motivation whether he believes that he is merely an accidental, albeit amazing, conglomeration of particles of matter, which, like grass, grows for a time and then withers and dies, or that he has been created in the Image of God with a vocation in this life and an eternal destiny beyond.

[1] Gordon W. Allport, *Pattern and Growth in Personality* (New York: Holt, Rinehart & Winston, Inc., 1961), pp. 561, 563.
[2] *Ibid.*, p. 550.

Much of the materialistic emphasis is understandable when one considers the background in the natural sciences which comprises the education of the medically trained psychiatrist, who, in one sense, sets the pace for psychotherapy. The majority of his preparation lies in the fields of physics and chemistry, physiology and neurology, comparative zoology, histology, cytology, and endocrinology. Even his premedical liberal arts background is crowded with essential mathematical and scientific prerequisites. His psychiatric residency is largely clinical, and opportunities to ask philosophical and sociological questions come "too little and too late." This is an unfortunate consequence of the technical-knowledge explosion. Even at best, he must skim over these fields in order not to become out-dated in the many disciplines that make up modern medicine.

The great error of naturalism, determinism, and materialism, as with most heresies, is not that they are totally lacking in useful insights and explanations, but that they offer partial answers yet claim to be comprehensive. The opposite of naturalism, Christian Science and certain esoteric mysticisms which deny or underrate nature and matter, are also incomplete, we need to see the picture "whole." Likewise, the reference to the materialistic background underlying medical training is not intended to be derogatory. But when confronted by moral and behavioral problems, it is vital to go beyond biochemistry and neurology to encompass the complete man; and this is beyond the philosophical scope of naturalism, determinism, and materialism.

The practical implications of these philosophies are quickly apparent when questions of ethical decisions arise. "What *ought* this patient to do next?" "*Should* we operate or not?" "Is it *best* for this unmarried girl to place her baby for adoption?" Very practical consequences flow out of any philosophy. Since the advent of Naziism and Communism, few serious persons would say that what one believes is not important.

Moral relativism has had increasing acceptance because of the emphasis put on psychology, anthropology, and sociology in the social sciences. In an accredited psychology clinic, a case was presented, as part of the training of students and for evaluation by colleagues, of a woman who had married in her early twenties, had begun an extensive series of infidelities, had been divorced and remarried, seemed confused about where to turn next, tried to seduce the therapist, and wondered if she should try going to a famous race-track resort area where she might finally meet a man with whom she could be "compatible." As the case unfolded many medical details were given concerning her birth, childhood diseases, and physical and psycho-sexual development. Her educational and familial history were thoroughly studied. But when the chief psychologist was asked about her religious affiliation and moral development, he seemed puzzled. When asked if such information would not shed light on such a client's confusion in making clear decisions concerning her ethical choices and future goals, the comment was, "Yes, I guess so. I don't know why we don't include such data in our case records. It must have something to do with the separation of church and state" (since the clinic was supported by tax funds). The trouble was not too much *scientific method,* but rather that given certain philosophical and ethical presuppositions, the final picture was of necessity, partial, and, in this case, lacking data in the most crucial area, both diagnostically and therapeutically.

Individualism may well be set over against commitment

to a community of interest. Rugged individualism assumes that the individual is neither responsible to nor in need of other persons. Philip Rieff maintains that the psychoanalytic type of therapy is the very opposite of "commitment therapy":

> The details of the psychoanalytic therapy bear out its informative and neutral, rather than transformative and committed character. It is, moreover, suited best to individuals who want to preserve their individualism, in the Tocquevillean sense, but have not quite come to terms with themselves in the solitude of their own hearts. Thus analytic therapy appeals to persons already living in a highly individualistic and democratic culture, like the American. The mechanism of confirming and strengthening democratic individualism is best seen in two aspects of the analytic relation: the transference, and the fee.[3]

Freud assumed that society, full of discontent and illusion, was not really worth committing oneself to. After all it was the harsh demands of civilized society which had so frustrated the instincts and drives of the patient as to make him sick in the first place. Some forms of negativistic existentialism (or perhaps misunderstood existentialism) put the individual above society and make it irrelevant whether the individual is ever reconciled with his neighbor or not. He can supposedly achieve his own unique integrity without the help of community. He is self-sufficient.

Hedonism is another characteristic of this ethic. In this philosophy pleasure and sensual satisfaction are the individual's chief "good" and are ends in themselves. Frequently this concept misleads therapist and client alike to regard the

---

[3] Philip Rieff, "A Schema of Therapeutic Types." A paper presented at the 1961 meeting of the American Psychological Association, New York City.

relief of symptoms as an adequate goal of therapy. The preva-
lence of hedonism as an ethical criterion may account for
the lack of what Florence Goodenough has called "frustration tolerance." There is no virtue in sacrifice, suffering, or
even exchanging long-term for short-term goals. *Self*-satisfac-
tion leads to deeply entrenched egocentrism and selfishness.
Although some have proposed an ethic of "enlightened self-
interest," it is this writer's experience that counselees who
have relied on self-interest have seldom gone beyond it. The
ethical obligation is quite different from that of Jesus cited
in Chapter 2—love God and your neighbor as yourself.

There is also a contrast in the two views of the *consequences* of the moral problem as viewed by the secular psychotherapist, and the consequences of sin as seen in the triad
of morality in the previous chapter.

Meaninglessness replaces the function of repentance or
contrition since there is no clear-cut verdict about "guilt."
Under the ethic of moral relativism, it is difficult to know
whether one has a problem, and still harder to know what
feeling would be appropriate if there were a problem. This
vague uncertainty the existentialists have called meaninglessness or "existential frustration." Frankl puts it this way:

> But in my opinion, man is neither dominated by the will-to-
> pleasure nor by the will-to-power, but by what I should like
> to call man's will-to-meaning. . . . Man is groping and long-
> ing for a meaning to be fulfilled by him alone; in other
> words, for what we could call a mission. . . .[4]

Here is a clarion call for the kind of anchorage that theology
used to provide. Man needs a purpose larger than himself,

[4] Viktor Frankl, *From Death-Camp to Existentialism* transl., Ilse Lasch
(Boston: Beacon Press, 1959), p. 97.

and an ethic higher than himself to challenge him to his full potentiality. Without this he has few guilts, few disappointments, few hopes; in fact he is stuck with a fate worse than guilt—nameless, faceless meaninglessness. He loses his humanness and adjusts to expectations of life more in line with those of the lower animals.

Irresponsibility is the natural result of combining an ethic of moral relativism with a deterministic view of social relations—it's hardly my fault if environmental forces beyond my control and irresistible *instinctual* drives *made me do it.* There is little need to confess my "sins" or to concern myself with restitution to society for the damage I have done to it. As in the ditty about the bird in the gilded cage, "she is more to be pitied than censured." And the height of self-pity (individualism makes it *self*-pity instead of social compassion) is illness, *self*-inflicted, hypochondriacal suffering.

Illness of this type is not to be compared with the suffering of martyrs and heroes who endure pain for some larger, social good. There is no sacrifice or service in such illness for it has as its cosmic orientation, simple meaninglessness; as its social orientation, self-centered individualism; and as its personal orientation, the "pleasure principle" of Hedonism. Many believe this to account for the tragic defeat of many Korean War prisoners who lacked the resources to stand against Communist "brain-washing." Unfortunately, a strictly secular approach to the moral problems of sin and guilt cannot and does not provide this resource.

Illness is the passive result of this approach. The client says in effect, "I'm helpless. Someone else must care for me. Since it was not my fault that I got into this mess, it is not my responsibility to get out." Secular psychotherapy, just because it is a *therapy,* offers a solution, albeit a solution quite different from that of the penance proposed in the previous chapter—contrition, confession, and satisfaction.

Scientific objectivity and detachment are strongly recommended by most schools of psychotherapy in preference to involvement. Although there are references to personal involvement such as in Freudian "transference" and Rogerian "empathy," the real solutions to the problem are not to be found in a personal faith relationship with the Creator, the love of God, and repentance for violating His will. The secular approach looks to the objectively verifiable data discovered in nature. Hence the stress on intellectual insight and education (or as some call therapy—"emotional re-education") and the motto "Know thyself" in the purely objective, factual sense. As Rieff indicated this is quite different from "commitment therapy" to which the dynamic of *faith* is essential. The criticism most feared by secular psychotherapists is not that they fail in healing but that they may be unscientific or lacking in objectivity.

The writer has the highest regard for appropriate scientific research and would agree that we *know* far too little about human behavior, mental illness, and psychotherapy. It is not that scientific objectivity is bad; it is indeed on the contrary essential. The error lies in trying to derive from it an adequate and final "theology" to account for the cosmic dimension within which man lives. Science has been assigned metaphysical and philosophical tasks which are beyond its scope and function. Given an adequate theology and a comprehensive enough philosophy to undergird it, there need be no limit to the amount of scientific investigation; but this would call for a change of emphasis; placing all other sciences once again under the queenly rule of theology. Would a secularist be willing?

Permissiveness characterizes secular therapy under the social dimension and replaces the former approach of "judgment." One doesn't feel justified in exercising judgment over one who is a helpless victim of circumstances, nor would one imprison those who are suffering from illness. In some ways this changed attitude has seemed to work great social reforms: mental patients were no longer thrown into snake pits nor, supposedly, beaten and abused; stigma was removed from various social violations such as illegitimacy and venereal disease (euphemistically referred to as a "social disease"— athlete's foot is also a social disease); distinctions between the genius and the feeble-minded were de-emphasized in ungraded classes, the withholding of academic grades, or by not "failing" those who did not "pass" in school. A great many formerly shameful conditions have become "nothing to be ashamed of." But this has been done on the basis of an amoral permissiveness rather than on the basis of some great forgiving love of neighbor. One "accepts" his neighbor because it doesn't really matter what he does. This is quite different from desiring actively to restore one's neighbor to social reconciliation in spite of his alienation and sin. This latter calls for active *love* of neighbor rather than permissive acceptance. It also calls for holding him morally responsible, but esteeming him of inestimable worth as a person created in the Image of God. Indeed he is restored to society through *confession* of responsibility—"It is my most grievous fault."

Permissiveness has a peculiar way of backfiring, because we still do discriminate in practice. The false hopes engendered by saying everyone is entitled to an education are crushed when the student who never "failed" does fail in his vocation; when the person who is reassured that his social violations do not really stigmatize him finds out in later

life that it does indeed *matter*. Permissiveness may turn out
to have far-reaching implications for delinquent and criminal
recidivism, as well as for the unmotivated mental patient.

Catharsis is the medical corollary of permissiveness, and
insight the personal application of scientific objectivity. The
fact that the mentally ill are called "sick" assumes a lack of
personal responsibility (see Chapter 4, "Patient or Penitent").
When this notion is combined with the ethic of Hedonism
it becomes clear that there is a great distinction between
catharsis and confession. Catharsis is frequently referred to
as "getting it off your chest" or "blowing off steam" or "venti-
lating" for one's own good. If there is a concern for neighbor
here, it is incidental; the primary concern is to make the
patient "feel better," to handle *his* frustrations, and alleviate
his anxiety. Frequently this leads to antisocial and hostile
relations with others, which is not surprising if the Ego is
considered independent of community.

The triad of morality according to medieval theology
(and hopefully again in contemporary theology) assumed that
the individual is of inestimable worth. In fact the angels in
Heaven rejoice over the rescue of one sinner. But it is never
man in isolation, rather it is assumed that there is no salvation outside of the Church (*extra Ecclesiam nulla salus*),
outside of the "household of faith." Again we return to the
threefold relationship without which man cannot be restored
to his full potentiality, his true nature in the Image of God.

The dilemma of the secular psychotherapist is that he tries
to accomplish an enormous task of personal reconciliation
with an inadequate and incomplete theory of the nature of
the universe, of society, and of the individual person. His
approach to the moral problem is neither comprehensive,

radical, or thoroughgoing enough; it is palliative and amelio-
rative when it must be reconstructive and transformative.

One shouldn't criticize secular therapies without offering
a workable alternative; nor should the alternative neglect
any of the valid insights of scientific investigation. The
churches have not used their full resources to deal with sin
and guilt, and should, therefore, be humble in their criticism. In Chapter 7 the question of how the confessional can
be made functional once again will be dealt with. But a little
more attention must be focused on the person caught in the
web of sin who must deal with the problem of guilt.

4

PATIENT
OR PENITENT

The role in which a person perceives himself will greatly
influence how he reacts to his situation in life. For example,
two roommates in a hospital are incapacitated by a physical
or mental illness. One considers himself the victim of an
impersonal disease over which he has little or no control;
the other views himself as a sinner who is receiving just re-
ward for his evil life. Such a basic difference in viewpoint
has profound implications for diagnosis of the disease, responsibility for the cure, type of therapy to be used, the
locus of the problem, as well as for the question of one's
philosophy of life.

Symptoms—the Amplified
and Distorted Voice of Conscience

It is now a commonplace that negative and antisocial emotions or actions can be the cause or precipitating factor in a wide variety of physical and mental symptoms. There have been many estimates as to the percentage of an average physician's patients who have functional rather than primarily organic difficulties.

In her *Psychiatry in the Medical Specialties,* Dunbar says:

> It has been found that at least 65 per cent of patients are suffering from illness syndromes initiated or seriously complicated by psychological problems.[1]

The Joint Commission on Mental Illness and Health has found that:

> Nearly all doctors reported a considerable number of mentally ill or emotionally disturbed patients. Several doctors estimated that as many as 75 per cent of their patients were emotionally disturbed.[2]

With careful definition of terms and the statistical tabulation of sufficient case data, it should be possible to be more exact concerning the nature and extent of the psychosomatic prob-

[1] Flanders Dunbar, *Psychiatry in the Medical Specialties* (New York: McGraw-Hill Book Company, Inc., 1959), p. v. See also chap. 1, "Changing Concept of Disease." Cf. O. Spurgeon English, and Gerald H. J. Pearson, *Emotional Problems of Living,* rev. ed. (New York: W. W. Norton and Company, Inc., 1955), "Psychophysiologic Disorders," pp. 490-492.

[2] Reginald Robinson, David F. Demarche, and Mildred K. Wagle, *Community Resources in Mental Health* (New York: Basic Books, Inc., 1960) "The Nonpsychiatric Physician," pp. 301-303.

lem in both private medical practice and in the general medical-surgical hospital. The hospital chaplain would be the logical one to be involved in such research.

There have been many attempts to correlate the moral and religious factors in a patient's life with the nature and meaning of his symptoms.[3] No one claims that 100 per cent of illnesses are functional, but the tendency in recent years is to look suspiciously at an increasing number. Guilt-producing behavior, negative emotions, etc., tend to throw the body into a precarious position, to disturb necessary homeostasis, and to make the person more susceptible to the ravages of germs and bacteria, which up to this time have been kept under control by various natural barriers. Thus Dunbar even includes accidents in the "three illness groups" together with cardiovascular disease and cancer.[4] When an "accident prone" patient has a need to punish himself for his past life, the question of morals and values comes urgently to the fore.

Simmons raises the question of the psychosomatic aspects of cancer.[5] When an excessive amount of certain hormones is produced, they bombard body tissue with carcinogenic elements, according to him. He would like to see more research into the etiology of cancer from a functional point of view. Cancerous deaths are 75 per cent higher in heavy smokers than among non-smokers. He raises the question whether

[3] See David Belgum, *Why Did It Happen To Me?* (Minneapolis: Augsburg Publishing House, 1960), Chapter 1, in which is discussed the insights into stress. See also Hans Selye, *The Stress of Life* (New York: McGraw-Hill Book Company, Inc., 1956), "General Adaptation Syndrome." See also Granger E. Westberg, *Minister and Doctor Meet* (New York: Harper and Row, Publishers, 1961), Chap. 6. Aarne Siirals goes further and states that mental illness, in particular, says something about the morality and conscience of the community. It is a symptom of a sick society. "The Meaning of Illness," *Journal of Religion and Health*, Vol. 1, No. 2, January, 1962, pp. 153-164.

[4] Dunbar, *loc. cit.*

[5] Harold E. Simmons, *The Psychosomatic Aspects of Cancer* (Washington, D. C.: Peabody Press, 1956).

excessive smoking may not be a crude gauge of the amount of emotional stress under which the person is trying to live. Perhaps that is the variable rather than the specific noxious agents in the tobacco itself. Anger and fear, according to Simmons, also flood the body with hormones containing carcinogenic elements.

It is, however, in the enormous field of mental illness that some of the sharpest distinctions may have to be drawn between patient and penitent. Can it be that many neurotic and psychotic symptoms are also the amplified and distorted voice of conscience? An increasing number of reputable psychotherapists are becoming discouraged about the psychoanalytic interpretation of mental illness and its various modifications in psychiatric practice; Eysenck, Szasz, and Mowrer, to mention a few.[6] Eysenck finds no scientific or statistical evidence for the efficacy of psychotherapy as it is generally practiced today. Szasz denies the term "mental illness" calling it a "myth." And Mowrer believes that neurotics and psychotics (barring any organic involvement) are not "sick," but "sinners" caught and condemned by their own consciences.

Mowrer's theory has already been tested on a small scale by Peterson[7] of the University of Illinois and Swensen[8] of the University of Tennessee. As it turns out, Mowrer's hypothesis is easily tested, as Swensen indicates:

[6] H. J. Eysenck, ed., *Handbook of Abnormal Psychology* (New York: Basic Books, Inc., 1961), Chap. 18. Thomas S. Szasz, *The Myth of Mental Illness* (New York: Harper and Row, Publishers, 1961). O. Hobart Mowrer, *The Crisis in Psychiatry and Religion* (New York: D. Van Nostrand Co., Inc., 1961).

[7] Donald R. Peterson, "The Insecure Child: Over-Socialized or Under-Socialized?" A mimeographed paper issued at the University of Illinois, 1961.

[8] Clifford H. Swensen Jr., "Sexual Behavior and Psychopathology: A Test of Mowrer's Hypothesis." A mimeographed paper issued at the University of Tennessee, January 12, 1962.

If Mowrer's contention is correct, one would expect people
who seek psychotherapy for neurotic complaints to have violated moral laws more frequently than normal people coming
from the same socio-economic background. . . . A group of
25 co-eds who had entered psychotherapy were compared
with a control group of 25 co-eds who were matched with
them according to age and school class. It was found that
the group needing psychotherapy had engaged in significantly less social activity but had had more extensive sexual
experience than the control group. Within the control
group itself, it was found that the girls who had had sexual
intercourse had significantly more psychosomatic problems
than the girls who had not engaged in sexual intercourse.[9]

Surely this is a question for research and should be studied
on a large scale in various settings. The results could help
answer the question: Should the incapacitated person play
the role of the patient or the penitent? If his symptoms are
the amplified and distorted voice of conscience, the answer is
quite obvious.

Guilt and Responsibility

Our generation may well be characterized
as an age of *irresponsibility*. Rather than accepting our guilt
for misdeeds, we rationalize our way out, blaming "condi-
tioned" causes; we attribute our behavior to our environment
or heredity, or to our faulty training or lack of need-gratifica-
tion. A nation-wide survey conducted by the Joint Commission on Mental Illness and Health discovered the following:

Despite the fact that it seems to take an unusual degree of
insight for an individual to admit that he needs help with a

[9] *Op. cit.,* pp. 1, 6.

mental or emotional problem, only about one-fourth of those who sought assistance traced their problems back to their own inadequacies with any clarity . . . few were prepared to be told that they must accept at least a share of the responsibility for their problems and that they must change themselves accordingly.[10]

A man nearing middle life had been the private patient of a psychiatrist and had also been treated by a clinical psychologist. He had been told that the reason he felt a compulsive need to abuse his wife verbally and physically was that he was expressing symbolically his hatred for a hostile and unloving stepmother. The pastor-counselor to whom he came for help despaired of going through the long catharsis which would have brought the two of them once again to the "insight" that the stepmother was the *cause* of his problem. So against his better judgment, he decided to confront him simply with the question of responsibility.

The minister asked, "On the last occasion when you beat your wife, if she had called the sheriff, what would the charges have been, if any?"

The client replied, "I don't think she ever would—as a matter of fact it never occurred to me. But I guess she would have a case; the charge would be assault and battery."

The next question was supremely naive, and only because there was a good relationship between them, no one laughed. The counselor simply asked, "And who would be tried and sent to the workhouse for thirty days? You or your stepmother?"

The interview moved rapidly onward and centered around the matter of guilt and its ensuing responsibility. It

[10] Joint Commission on Mental Illness and Health, *Action for Mental Health* (New York: Basic Books, Inc., 1961), p. 103.

turned out that there was much to feel guilty about, much of it for which he acknowledged responsibility. It became increasingly less realistic or useful for him to use his dead stepmother for a scapegoat.

Since Freud we have assumed that "insight" into the forces that have molded our personalities is a good and health-producing experience. The goal has been the age-old proverb: "Know thyself." However, the irony of it has been that, many times it has led to the "insight" that it is someone else's fault that we have turned out as we have and that we act or feel as bad as we do. The longer we have talked in therapy the longer has grown the list of those culprits who are *responsible* for our disordered lives.

One of the clichés in the mental-health field has been that mental illness is nothing to be ashamed of because it is simply an illness like any physical illness. But psychosomatic medicine has taken the comfort out of that reassurance, for, if the message is clear, ulcers, arthritis, some cardio-vascular diseases, etc., may very well be matters about which to be ashamed (excluding obvious organicity). Neurotic and psychotic breakdown may be an involuntary confession of guilt, just as many somatic symptoms are the amplified and distorted voice of conscience. The appropriate action for one so stricken would be penitence in the face of guilt, rather than a plea of irresponsible illness.

The opposite of acceptance of responsibility for one's life is paranoid projection—attributing blame and responsibility to others or to the outside environment. In this sense, the paranoid patient is sicker than the one who is sunk into a deep depression. The latter at least knows he has a problem and that it is *his* problem.

During Professor Mowrer's Seminar at the University of

Illinois, the following operational definition was evolved: "If a person has done something that he is afraid to have known, he is guilty." This brings us to the clear-cut division between those who are publicly declared to be guilty and those who are surreptitiously guilty, but camouflaging it under the guise of mental or psychosomatic illness.

The Hospital Patient
and the Penitentiary Inmate

Everyone agrees that the penitentiary inmate should be penitent. Public disgrace is a great aid in this spiritual exercise, although some hardened criminals are not penitent because they have an underdeveloped, squelched, or atrophied conscience. In psychological parlance, they are psychopathic because they lack an adequate Super Ego; they have not been adequately socialized.

But what of those who have done wrong, who have violated their own conscience and the demands of society, but have not been caught? Some inexorable sense of moral homeostasis, some built-in sense of justice seems to take over, and they punish themselves with a six- to twelve-month sentence of psychotic depression, frightening hallucinations, or other morbid mental states. Or they may choose one of a dozen or more psychosomatic symptoms.

Those who use the cliché referred to above, that mental illness is nothing to be ashamed of, will chide me for being harsh and judgmental toward patients who have suffered enough already. But I should like someday to see the mental-hospital patients and the psychosomatic patients compared with penitentiary inmates, case history by case history, for I suspect that their behavior and their characters are quite similar. My own experience has not been broad enough to give a reliable answer; but it has been varied enough to raise some questions.

Why is it that in clinical-pastoral training in hospital ministry so much effort is directed toward helping the student-chaplains to overcome their shock, their amazement and surprise at what they hear from the patient's record, or, in mental hospitals, what is revealed at staff meetings? At present some of us are working at a state mental research hospital with a group of psychotic women. In the over twenty that have passed through the group or remain in it, there is represented theft, adultery, homosexuality, incest, masturbation and assorted perversions, beating and strangling of children (short of murder), criminal abortion, alcoholism, lying and other forms of dishonesty, rejection of responsibility concerning familial or vocational duties, temper tantrums as well as physical violence—just to mention a few things from memory. The question is: would case histories from the penitentiary sound much different? These are persons who were not apprehended by an officer of the law, but who were caught by their own consciences and who punished themselves by various forms of psychic and social misery.

The differences between the hospital and penitentiary groups have recently been made to appear less distinct, the contrast less great. In many ways the increased use of psychological and psychiatric services in penal institutions has been based on the assumption that the criminal offender is suffering from some form of mental illness. His crime is a symptom and should be treated more or less medically. Juvenile delinquency appears to some to be more of a sickness than a sin. According to this trend, it is less and less likely that one would come across a bona fide penitent, but increasingly likely that one would discover patients, whether suffering from physical, mental, or social diseases. Criminals would be "hospitalized" for their anti-social sickness.

It is the contention of the line of argument outlined above that there may indeed be less difference between the hospital and penitentiary groups, but for exactly the opposite reason. Namely, the psychosomatic patients and the mentally ill have as much to be penitent about as the penitentiary or criminal group. All three groups have violated the moral demands of society, and have alienated themselves from society; the social accident of having been publicly apprehended turns out to be psychologically as well as ethically incidental. They all suffer one way or another as long as this condition of disobedience and alienation remains unresolved.

In medieval times it was not uncommon to speak quite openly about the consequences of sins. The "Penitential Handbooks" were in some ways crude, but in other ways more perceptive than are we in our abnegation of personal responsibility.[11] If man is in any genuine sense responsible for his behavior, we will have to reverse some of our attitudes about his misconduct. Men will have to face more realistically and more humanly the consequences of their sins. If a man burns with hatred for his boss for ten years, covets his wife, and plots against him at the office, it may turn out to be scientifically unsophisticated to say with surprise, "I can't imagine what hit me," when he becomes incapacitated with arthritis or sinks into a deep psychotic depression. Therapy which gives him a combination of hormones and tranquilizers will not be thorough enough; nor will the hospital

[11] John T. McNeill and Helena M. Gamer, *Medieval Handbooks of Penance* (New York: Columbia University Press, 1938). See also Thomas Pollock Oakley, *English Penitential Discipline and Anglo-Saxon Law in Their Joint Influence* (New York: Columbia University Ph.D. dissertation, 1923).

chaplain have fulfilled his function when he has counseled him to the point where he has "insight" into the combination of interpersonal influences in his personality development that *made* him do it, say it, or wish it.

What Then Is the Role of the Minister of Religion?

In proportion as it becomes scientifically demonstrable that symptoms are often the amplified voice of conscience, it should become logically inescapable that the religious agencies which *inform* conscience have the function of restoring those persons who have run afoul of their consciences. The church has called this many things: a few being "binding up the brokenhearted," "the ministry of reconciliation," and "the cure of souls."

Such a ministry may well have as its function helping many afflicted people to discover, or rather acknowledge, that they are not victims of an impersonal and amoral disease, but that their illness has a moral and theological perspective that is of vital importance to them. Many people have not suffered from illness, per se, but they are sick (some sick unto death) of the kind of life they have lived and the interpersonal relationships they have destroyed.

Acknowledging psychosomatic and mental illnesses as a chastisement for guilt can have a positive aspect. It means that one still has conscience and character enough to be bothered by wrong-doing and is sensitive to the moral demands of one's fellow men. One has not passed beyond the pale into that total lack of moral concern, which is dangerously close to, if indeed not, the "sin against the Holy Spirit."

Who else can operate competently in this vital ministry

if not the clergy of the Church and the chaplains that minister in our hospitals? What other point of view can handle this issue if not a theology which is aware of the problem of sin and which stands ready to deal effectively with the ravages of guilt? And the test of such a ministry of reconciliation may well be whether persons dodging responsibility under the guise of psychosomatic or mental illness will exchange their role of patient for penitent.

5

WHAT WAS
AVAILABLE IN THE CHURCHES?

Many ask, "What can the churches do about mental health?" At present the churches are helping through pastoral counseling programs, church-sponsored mental health clinics, and indications of co-operation between clergymen and psychiatrists. This chapter asks the question in a little different way. Assuming that the discussion in the previous chapters has been correct in relating sin and guilt to various aspects of mental illness, the question must be raised in terms of the resources the churches have said that they have available for dealing with the problem.

Before we propose any grand *new* plan, it is necessary to ascertain what plans have already been tried. Have they been given a fair trial? Perhaps valid and appropriate methods have fallen into disuse or disrepute. Chapters 5 and 6 deal with the churches' indigenous methods of pastoral care and discipline, and their attempts to restore the sinner to wholeness and community so that he can function as God intended.

The aim of the present chapter is to present briefly and without editorial comment succinct statements of the historic positions, principles, and methods of seven denominations concerning the problem of guilt. Chapter 6 will assay whether or not these methods are being used extensively at the present time by these denominations, together with an estimate of their effectiveness as judged by clergymen of each denomination.

The seven denominations are: Eastern Orthodox, Roman Catholic, Anglican (Episcopal), Lutheran, Presbyterian, Methodist, and Baptist. An analysis of whether or not clergymen of these denominations judged the statements cited as being either authoritative or representative of their own denominations will be presented in Chapter 6.

The Eastern Orthodox Church's Position on Penance

The doctrinal positions of the Orthodox Church are contained in the seven General Ecumenical Councils, held from 325 through 787 A.D. Cited as authorities are the teachings of the early Church Fathers such as St. Athanasius, St. Ambrose, St. Basil, and St. John Chrysostom. "The sources of the Orthodox Faith are Holy Tradition and Holy Scriptures."[1]

[1] Stephen H. R. Upson, *Orthodoxy, Protestantism and Roman Catholicism* (a booklet) (Bridgeville, Pennsylvania: Orthodox Catholic Literature Association, 1958), p. 4.

". . . the essential conditions for absolution are penitence
and confession only, and these are absolutely indispensable
for receiving remission of sins, which is conveyed only by
the priest. He may assign penances, but they are beneficial
and remedial, and may never be considered as conditions of
absolution, or as its completion." [2]

"For man to be worthy of so great a love by which God
gave His only begotten Son to save us from sin and perdition
is almost superhuman. It could not be, had not our Lord
instituted also the Mystery of Holy Penance when He told
us to confess our sins to each other and gave His Apostles
the power to remit sins. 'Receive ye the Holy Spirit; whosoever sins ye remit, they are remitted unto them, and whosoever sins ye retain, they are retained.' (John 20:22-23)

"Every sin we commit against man, we commit against
God, too. There is no sin that does not hurt God. It is not
sufficient to confess and make retribution to the person injured. But we should seek also to confess to a priest, succes-
sor to the Holy Apostles, who have spiritually inherited the
power to forgive sins. There are sins for which there appears, to human understanding, to be no forgiveness. Yet we
know of many instances of great sinners who through true
repentance had their sins remitted, and have become great
saints.

"The Church urges frequent confession, especially before
Holy Communion and during illness, so that the soul may
ever be ready to stand before the Judgment Seat. In no way
is this a control of the faithful's lives by the priesthood. The
priest is only the channel through which men gain God's forgiveness. One does not confess to the priest as a person, but

---

[2] Frank Gavin, *Some Aspects of Contemporary Greek Orthodox Thought*
(Milwaukee, Wisconsin: Morehouse Publishing Co., 1923), p. 370. (See whole
section on "Penance," pp. 358-370.)

to God through the priest. The priest is there to help the penitent formulate his sin and to be the visible transmitter of God's grace of forgiveness. He is the vehicle which Christ instituted for this purpose." [3]

THE ORDER OF CONFESSION [4]

The Order is to be preceded by preparation. "In order that you may make a good confession, it is necessary for you to prepare yourself carefully. Ask God to give you grace to make a thorough examination of your conscience, courage to make a sincere and complete confession, and strength to amend your way of life in the days to come."

"Self-Examination" consists in reviewing the Ten Commandments as criteria by which to judge one's sins.

The Order of Confession
[A short form]

While the Penitent is waiting for the Priest to hear his confessions he says quietly the "Trisagion Prayers" and Psalm 50, if he has time, and then aloud:

I have sinned, O Lord God: forgive me. O God, be gracious unto me a sinner.

When the Penitent's turn comes, he goes forward and kneels in the proper place (before the Ikonostasis, at the front of the church, beside the Priest), and says aloud:

[3] H. R. H. Princess Ileana of Romania, *The Spirit of The Eastern Ortho-dox Church* (Advent Papers series) (Cincinnati: Forward Movement Publications, n. d.), pp. 15, 16.
[4] *A Pocket Prayer Book for Orthodox Christians* (Brooklyn, New York: Syrian Orthodox Archdiocese, 1956). See "Part Two, Prayers and Devotions for Confession and Holy Communion," pp. 37-46. Quotation of "The Order of Confession" itself is from pages 43-45.

O Father, Lord of heaven and earth, I confess to thee all the hidden and open sins of my heart and mind, which I have committed unto this present day; wherefore I be of thee, the righteous and compassionate Judge, remission of sins and grace to sin no more.

Then the Priest says in a kindly voice:

My brother, inasmuch as thou hast come to God, and to me, be not ashamed; for thou speakest not unto me, but unto God, before whom thou standest.

The priest questions the Penitent concerning his sins, and the questioning finished, he says these words:

My spiritual child, who hast confessed to my humble self, I, humble and a sinner, have not power on earth to forgive sins, but God alone; yet through that divinely spoken word which came to the Apostles after the Resurrection of our Lord Jesus Christ, saying: Whosoever sins ye remit, they are remitted, and whosoever sins ye retain, they are retained, we too are emboldened to say: Whatsoever thou hast said to my most humble self, and whatsoever thou hast not succeeded in saying, either through ignorance, or through forgetfulness, whatever it may be: God forgive thee in this present world, and in that which is to come.

(The Priest commonly, standing beside the kneeling Penitent, lays his stole upon the Penitent while pronouncing the Absolution.)

And the Priest adds this Prayer, making the sign of the Cross over the Penitent:

God it was who forgave David through Nathan the Prophet, when he confessed his sins, and Peter weeping bitterly for his denial, and the sinful woman in tears at his feet, and the Publican, and the Prodigal Son: May that same God forgive thee all things, through me a sinner, both in this present world, and in that which is to come, and set thee uncondemned before his dread Judgment Seat.

And the Priest adds:

And now, having no further care for the sins which thou hast declared, depart in peace.

Then the Priest allows the Penitent to depart with his blessing:

May Christ our true God, through the prayers of his most holy Mother and of all the Saints, have mercy upon us and save us, forasmuch as he is good and lovest mankind. Amen.

The Penitent returns to his seat and gives thanks to God for His goodness, saying one or more of the Prayers After Confession which follow:

O almighty and merciful God, I truly thank thee for the forgiveness of my sins; bless me, O Lord, and help me always, that I may ever do that which is pleasing to thee, and sin no more. Amen.

*The Roman Catholic Position on
and Practice of
Penance and Confession:*

[*According to the Council of Trent,* Session
14, Chapter 3—"On the parts, and on the
fruit of this Sacrament"]

"The holy synod doth furthermore teach, that the form of the sacrament of penance, wherein its force principally consists, is placed in those words of the minister, *I absolve thee,* etc.; to which words indeed certain prayers are, according to the custom of the holy Church, laudably joined, which nevertheless by no means regard the essence of that form, neither are they necessary for the administration of the sacrament itself. But the acts of the penitent himself, to wit, contrition, confession and satisfaction, are as it were the matter of this sacrament. Which acts, inasmuch as they are, by God's institution, required in the penitent for the integrity of the sacrament, and for the full and perfect remission of sins, are for this reason called the parts of penance. But the thing signified indeed and the effect of this sacrament, as far as regards its force and efficacy, is reconciliation with God, which sometimes, in persons who are pious and who receive this sacrament with devotion, is wont to be followed by peace and serenity of conscience, with exceeding consolation of spirit. The holy Synod, whilst delivering these things touching the parts and the effect of this sacrament, condemns at the same time the opinions of those who contend, that, the terrors which agitate the conscience, and faith, are the parts of penance."

"On Confession"—Session 14, Chapter 5

"From the institution of the sacrament of Penance as already explained, the universal Church has always understood, that the entire confession of sins was also instituted by the Lord, and is of divine right necessary for all who have fallen after baptism . . . in order that, in accordance with the power of the keys, they may pronounce the sentence of forgiveness or retention of sins. For it is manifest, that priests could not have exercised this judgment without knowledge of the cause; neither indeed could they have observed equity in enjoining punishments, if the said faithful should have declared their sins in general only, and not rather specifically, and one by one. Whence it is gathered that all mortal sins, of which, after diligent examination of themselves, they are conscious, must needs be by penitents enumerated in confession, even though those sins be most hidden, and committed only against the two last precepts of the decalogue,— sins which sometimes wound the soul more grievously, and are more dangerous, than those which are committed outwardly . . . . Now the very difficulty of a confession like this, and the shame of making known one's sins, might indeed seem a grievous thing, were it not alleviated by the so many and so great advantages and consolations, which are most assuredly bestowed by absolution upon all who worthily approach to this sacrament . . . ." [5]

"HOW TO GO TO CONFESSION" [6] [*This is a typical suggested form.*]

---

[5] *The Canons and Decrees of the Sacred and Oecumenical Council of Trent.* Trans. The Rev. J. Waterworth (London: C. Dolman, 1848), pp. 95, 97, 98.

[6] A tract reprinted from *Outlines of Catholic Teaching* by John J. Keating, C.S.P. (New York: The Paulist Press, 1955). For complete "Devotions for Confession" and more elaborate explanation, see *The New Roman Missal in Latin and English* by F. X. Lasance and Francis Augustine Walsh (New York: Benziger Brothers, Inc., 1950), pp. 1793-1798. See also: *Saint Andrew Daily Missal*, by Dom Gaspar Lefebvre (Saint Paul, Minnesota: The E. M. Lohmann Co., 1953), pp. 1104-1106.

Five steps for a Good Confession

1. Examine your conscience.
2. Be sincerely sorry for your sins.
3. Confess your sins.
4. Resolve to amend your life.
5. After your confession, do the penance the priest assigns.

Prayer Before Confession

O my God, help me to see and know the condition of my soul honestly and humbly, and to make a sincere and truthful confession. Teach me true sorrow for my sins. Then, in Thy mercy, grant me Thy forgiveness, Thy grace, and Thy love, through the infinite merits of Jesus Christ my Redeemer. Amen.

Examination of Conscience [a few of many examples cited]

Did I refuse to believe God's revelation?
Did I blaspheme God, swear, or curse?
Did I disobey or disrespect my parents or legitimate superiors?
Did I give a fair wage to my employee?
Did I give bad example, get drunk, fight or quarrel?
Did I deliberately perform impure acts by myself or with others?
Did I lie deliberately to deceive; injure others by lies . . . etc.?

Procedure in the Confessional

When the priest opens the slide begin by saying:

Bless me, Father, in this confession. It is—a week, a month (state the length of time)—since my last confession. I accuse myself of the following sins.

Then tell the sins and the number of times committed. When you have finished telling your sins, you should say:

For these and all the sins of my past life I am truly sorry.

Then wait while the priest gives any necessary advice and assigns the penance.

You recite the Act of Contrition:	While the priest gives the Absolution in Latin:*
O my God, I am heartily sorry for having offended Thee, and I detest all my sins, because I dread the loss of heaven and the pains of hell, but most of all because they offend Thee, my God, Who art all good and deserving of my love. I firmly resolve, with the help of Thy grace, to confess my sins, to do penance, and to amend my life. Amen.	May Our Lord Jesus Christ absolve thee, and I, by His authority, absolve thee from every bond of excommunication and interdict, according to my power and your need. Therefore, I absolve thee from thy sins, in the name of the Father and of the Son, and of the Holy Ghost. Amen.

* *An English translation of the Form of Absolution said by the priest to the penitent.*

The Anglican View
of Confession and Penance:
From The Articles of Religion:

"XVI. *Of Sin after Baptism.*

Not every deadly sin willingly committed after Baptism is sin against the Holy Ghost, and unpardonable. Wherefore the grant of repentance is not to be denied to such as fall into sin after Baptism. After we have received the Holy Ghost, we may depart from grace given, and fall into sin, and by the grace of God may arise again, and amend our lives. And therefore they are to be condemned, which say, they can no more sin as long as they live here, or deny the place of forgiveness to such as truly repent."

"XXXIII. *Of excommunicate Persons, how they are to be avoided.*

That person which by open denunciation of the Church is rightly cut off from the unity of the Church, and excommunicated, ought to be taken of the whole multitude of the faithful, as an Heathen and Publican, until he be openly reconciled by penance, and received into the Church by a Judge that hath authority thereunto." [7]

GENERAL RUBRICS FOR HOLY COMMUNION:

"If among those who come to be partakers of the Holy Communion, the Minister shall know any to be an open and

---

[7] *The Book of Common Prayer and Administration of the Sacraments and Other Rites and Ceremonies of the Church* (New York: The Church Pension Fund, 1945), pp. 605-606, 609. See a comparison of the early versions of 1552, 1562, and 1571 in Appendix III of *A History of the Articles of Religion,* Charles Hardwick (Cambridge: John Deighton, 1851). In the above passages and in the selections from the *Book of Common Prayer* following, the contemporary version is used for the convenience of the reader.

notorious evil liver, or to have done any wrong to his neighbours by word or deed, so that the Congregation be thereby
offended; he shall advertise him, that he presume not to come
to the Lord's Table, until he have openly declared himself to
have truly repented and amended his former evil life, that
the Congregation may thereby be satisfied; and that he hath
recompensed the parties to whom he hath done wrong; or at
least declare himself to be in full purpose to do so, as soon as
he conveniently may.

"The same order shall the Minister use with those,
betwixt whom he perceiveth malice and hatred to reign; not
suffering them to be partakers of the Lord's Table, until he
know them to be reconciled. And if one of the parties, so at
variance, be content to forgive from the bottom of his heart
all that the other hath trespassed against him, and to make
amends for that wherein he himself hath offended; and the
other party will not be persuaded to a godly unity, but remain
still in his forwardness and malice; the Minister in that case
ought to admit the penitent person to the Holy Communion,
and not him that is obstinate. Provided, That every Minister
so repelling any, as is herein specified, shall be obliged to give
an account of the same to the Ordinary, within fourteen days
after, at the farthest."

RUBRICS FOR THE ORDER FOR THE VISITATION OF THE SICK:

"Here may the Minister inquire of the sick person as to
his acceptance of the Christian faith, and as to whether he
repent him truly of his sins, and be in charity with all the
world; exhorting him to forgive, from the bottom of his heart,
all persons that have offended him; and if he hath offended
any other, to ask them forgiveness; and where he hath done

injury or wrong to any man, that he make amends to the uttermost of his power.

"Then shall the sick person be moved to make a special confession of his sins, if he feel his conscience troubled with any matter; after which confession, on evidence of his repentance, the Minister shall assure him of God's mercy and forgiveness." [8]

THE MANNER OF HEARING CONFESSIONS:[9]

"Confessions ought always to be heard in the Church proper, except in cases of necessity or grave inconvenience . . . . The Priest, vested in surplice and violet stole, sits in the accustomed place where confessions are heard. The penitent, kneeling beside him, says in a low tone:

Bless me, Father, for I have sinned.

The Priest responds:

The Lord be in thy heart and upon thy lips, that so thou mayest worthily confess all thy sins; In the Name of the Father, and of the Son, and of the Holy Ghost. Amen.

"The penitent then makes his Confession, using the following or a similar formula:

[8] *Ibid.*, pages 84-85 and 313. For the original version see *The Book of Common Prayer, Printed by Whitchurch March 1549. Commonly Called The First Book of Edward VI.* (London: William Pickering, 1844.) (This is a facsimile reprint.)

[9] *A Manual for Priests of the American Church* (Complementary to the Occasional Offices of the *Book of Common Prayer*) (Cambridge, Massachusetts: Society of Saint John the Evangelist, 1961), pp. 22-25.

I confess to Almighty God, to all the Saints, and to you,
Father, that I have sinned very much, in thought, word,
deed, and omission, by my own great fault. Since my last
confession which was (here he tells the Priest when it occurred), when I received absolution and performed my
penance, I have committed these sins:

He confesses his sins and continues:

For these and all other sins which I cannot now remember,
I am very sorry. I will try to do better, and I humbly ask
pardon of God; and of you Father, I ask for penance, advice
and absolution. Amen.

"After the Confession is ended, the Priest may address a
few words of counsel to the penitent, and will then assign a
suitable penance. For secret sins, however grave, public
penance must not be imposed, lest the Seal of the Confessional be violated thereby.

Penance having been enjoined and accepted, the Priest
shall say:

The Form of Absolution

Almighty God have mercy upon thee, forgive thee thy sins,
and bring thee to everlasting life. Amen.

Then, raising his right hand toward the penitent, but not
so as to be seen by anyone in the church, he continues:

The Almighty and merciful Lord grant thee pardon, absolution, and remission of thy sins. Amen.
Our Lord Jesus Christ, who hath left power to his Church
to absolve all sinners who truly repent and believe in him,

of his great mercy forgive thee thine offences: And by his authority committed unto me, I absolve thee from all thy sins,
In the Name of the Father, and of the Son, and of the Holy
Ghost. Amen. [From the English Prayer Book]
May the Passion of our Lord Jesus Christ make whatsoever
good thou hast done, or evil thou hast endured, be unto thee
for the forgiveness of sins, the increase of grace, and the re-
ward of eternal life: And the blessing of God Almighty, the
Father, the Son, and the Holy Ghost, be upon thee and
remain with thee always. Amen.
"Go in peace, the Lord hath put away all thy sins." ["and
pray for me a sinner" frequently added.]

Luther's View
of Confession and Penance

"The true way and the right method, with-
out which there is no other, is that most worthy, gracious, and
holy sacrament of penance, which God gave for the comfort
of all sinners when he gave the keys to St. Peter in behalf of
the whole Christian Church and, in Matthew 16:19, said,
'Whatever you bind on earth shall be bound in heaven, and
whatever you loose on earth shall be loosed in heaven.' This
holy, comforting, and gracious word of God must enter deeply
into the heart of every Christian, where he may with great
gratitude let it become part of him. For the sacrament of
penance consists in this: forgiveness of sin, comfort and peace
of conscience, besides joy and blessedness of heart over against
all sins and terrors of conscience, as well as against all despair
and assaults by the gates of hell (Matt. 16:18). . . .

"In confession, if a priest wishes to inquire, or if you want
to examine yourself, as to whether or not you are truly
contrite, I have no objection. Just so no one becomes so bold
in the sight of God that he claims to have sufficient contrition.

. . . . Actually in this sacrament the priest, in his word, brings God's message about sin and the forgiveness of guilt. Hence, he should indeed be the one who inquires and discerns most of all whether a person is receptive to the message. Such receptivity can never consist in anything other than faith and the desire to receive this message. Sin, contrition, and good works should be treated in sermons before the sacrament and confession. . . .

"Concerning satisfaction, let this now suffice: the best kind of satisfaction is to sin no more and to do all possible good toward your fellow-man, be he enemy or friend. This kind of satisfaction is rarely mentioned; we think to pay for everything simply through assigned prayers." [10]

"Penance also is to be reckoned as a sacrament—all sacraments are a kind of penance. There are other reasons too, for calling it a sacrament, but they need not be recounted here.

"Now we have already shown that it is necessary to preach penance, and to punish fearless behavior which is now in the world and has its origin, at least in part, in a wrong understanding of the faith. For many who hear that they should believe, so that all their sins will be forgiven, fashion their own faith and think they are pure. Thus they become secure and arrogant. Such carnal security is worse than all the errors hitherto prevailing. Therefore in preaching the gospel it is necessary in every way to instruct the people where faith may be found and how one attains it. For true faith cannot exist where there is not true contrition and true fear and terror before God. . . .

"Now penance in reality is sincere contrition and sorrow

---

[10] "The Sacrament of Penance" (a teaching sermon dated 1519) *Luther's Works, Word and Sacrament I,* Vol. 35. Ed. E. Theodore Bachmann, gen. ed. Helmut T. Lehmann, trans. E. Theodore Bachmann (Philadelphia: Muhlenberg Press, 1960), pp. 10, 11, 18, and 21 respectively.

over one's sins and sincere fear of the wrath and judgement of God. This is contrition and the acknowledgement of sin. 'Mortification of the flesh' is also, properly penance. So in the Scriptures contrition has many names . . . ." [11]

FROM LUTHER'S SMALL CATECHISM:

Confession and Absolution
How Plain People Are to Be Taught to Confess

What is confession?

Answer: Confession consists of two parts. One is that we confess our sins. The other is that we receive absolution or forgiveness from the confessor as from God himself, by no means doubting but firmly believing that our sins are thereby forgiven before God in heaven.

What sins should we confess?

Answer: Before God we should acknowledge that we are guilty of all manner of sins, even those of which we are not aware, as we do in the Lord's Prayer. Before the confessor, however, we should confess only those sins of which we have knowledge and which trouble us.

What are such sins?

Answer: Reflect on your condition in the light of the Ten Commandments: whether you are a father or mother, a son or daughter, a master or servant; whether you have been disobedient, unfaithful, lazy, ill-tempered, or quarrelsome;

---

[11] "Instructions for the Visitors of Parish Pastors in Electoral Saxony" (dated 1528) *Luther's Works, Church and Ministry* II, Vol. 40. trans. by Conrad Bergendoff, Ed. E. Theodore Bachmann, Gen. Ed. Helmut T. Lehmann (Philadelphia: Muhlenberg Press, 1958), pp. 293, 294 and 296 respectively. Note: See Luther's "The Keys," a treatise written in 1530, for his criticism of "the horrible abuse and misunderstanding of the precious keys." *Ibid.* Vol. 40:325-377. See also Articles 11 and 25 concerning "Confession" in "The Augsburg Confession," pp. 34 and 61-63 respectively, *The Book of Concord*, ed. Theodore G. Tappert (Philadelphia: Muhlenberg Press, 1959).

whether you have harmed anyone by word or deed; and whether you have stolen, neglected, or wasted anything, or done other evil.

Please give me a brief form of confession.

Answer: You should say to the confessor: "Dear Pastor, please hear my confession and declare that my sins are forgiven for God's sake."

"Proceed."

"I, a poor sinner, confess before God that I am guilty of all sins. In particular I confess in your presence that, as a manservant or maidservant, etc. I am unfaithful to my master, for here and there I have not done what I was told. I have made my master angry, caused him to curse, neglected to do my duty, and caused him to suffer loss. I have also been immodest in word and deed. I have quarreled with my equals. I have grumbled and sworn at my mistress, etc. For all this I am sorry and pray for grace. I mean to do better."

A master or mistress may say: "In particular I confess in your presence that I have not been faithful in training my children, servants, and wife to the glory of God. I have cursed. I have set a bad example by my immodest language and actions. I have injured my neighbor by speaking evil of him, overcharging him, giving him inferior goods and short measure." Masters and mistresses should add whatever else they have done contrary to God's commandments and to their action in life, etc.

If, however, anyone does not feel that his conscience is burdened by such or by greater sins, he should not worry, nor should he search for and invent other sins, for this would turn confession into torture; he should simply mention one or two sins of which he is aware. For example, "In particular I confess that I once cursed. On one occasion I also spoke indecently. And I neglected this or that," etc. Let this suffice.

If you have knowledge of no sin at all (which is quite unlikely), you should mention none in particular, but receive forgiveness upon the general confession which you make to God in the presence of the confessor.

Then the confessor shall say: "God be merciful to you and strengthen your faith. Amen."

Again he shall say: "Do you believe that the forgiveness I declare is the forgiveness of God?"

Answer: "Yes, I do."

Then he shall say: "Be it done for you as you have believed. According to the command of our Lord Jesus Christ, I forgive you your sins in the name of the Father and of the Son and of the Holy Spirit. Amen. Go in peace."

A confessor will know additional passages of the Scriptures with which to comfort and to strengthen the faith of those whose consciences are heavily burdened or who are distressed and sorely tried. This is intended simply as an ordinary form of confession for plain people." [12]

THE BOOK OF CONCORD: THE AUGSBURG CONFESSION (1530)

Article XI

"Our churches teach that private absolution should be retained in the churches. However, in confession an enumeration of all sins is not necessary, for this is not possible according to the Psalm, 'Who can discern his errors?' (Ps. 19:12)." [13]

---

[12] "The Small Catechism of Dr. Martin Luther" (1529) (The section quoted is dated 1531) *The Book of Concord,* ed. by Theodore G. Tappert (Philadelphia: Muhlenberg Press, 1959), pp. 349-351.
[13] *Ibid.,* p. 34.

Article XXV

"Confession has not been abolished in our churches, for it it is not customary to administer the body of Christ except to those who have previously been examined and absolved. The people are very diligently taught concerning faith in connection with absolution, a matter about which there has been profound silence before this time. Our people are taught to esteem absolution highly because it is the voice of God and is pronounced by God's command. The power of keys is praised, and people are reminded of the great consolation it brings to terrified consciences, are told that God requires faith to believe such absolution as God's own voice heard from heaven . . . . The marginal note in *De Poenitentia* (Chrysostom) Dist. 5, in the chapter 'Consideret,' admits that such confession is of human right. Nevertheless, confession is retained among us on account of the great benefit of absolution and because it is otherwise useful to consciences." [14]

THE SMALCALD ARTICLES (1537)

Article VII

"The keys are a function and power given to the church by Christ to bind and loose sins, not only the gross and manifest sins but also those which are subtle and secret and which God alone perceives . . . ." [15]

Article VIII

"Since absolution or the power of the keys, which was instituted by Christ in the Gospel, is a consolation and help against sin and a bad conscience, confession and absolution should by no means be allowed to fall into disuse in the

[14] *Ibid.,* pp. 61-64.
[15] *Ibid.,* p. 311.

church, especially for the sake of timid consciences and for
the sake of untrained young people who need to be examined
and instructed in Christian doctrine . . . ." [16]

Calvin on Confession
and Discipline

John Calvin has many harsh words for pen-
ance and "auricular" and "compulsory" confession; here are
cited only a few references which indicate how he felt the
functions of confession and church discipline might be legitimately carried out.

Book III, Chapter IV, Article 12

"Private confession in the cure of souls"

"Scripture, moreover, approves two forms of private confession: one made for our own sake, to which the statement of
James refers that we should confess our sins to one another
(James 5:16) . For he means that disclosing our weaknesses to
one another, we help one another with mutual counsel and
consolation. The other form we are to use for our neighbor's
sake, to appease him and to reconcile him to us if through
fault of ours he has been in any way injured. And in the first
kind of confession, even though James, by not expressly determining on whose bosom we should unburden ourselves,
leaves us free choice to confess to that one of the flock of the
church who seems most suitable. Yet we must also preferably
choose pastors inasmuch as they should be judged especially
qualified above the rest. Now I say that they are better fitted
than the others because the Lord has appointed them by the

---

[16] *Ibid.*, p. 312.

very calling of the ministry to instruct us by word of mouth to overcome and correct our sins, and also to give us consolation through assurance of pardon (Matt. 16:19; 18:18; John 20:23). For while the duty of mutual admonition and rebuke is entrusted to all Christians, it is especially enjoined upon ministers. Thus, although all of us ought to console one another and confirm one another in assurance of divine mercy, we see that the ministers themselves have been ordained witnesses and sponsors of it to assure our consciences of forgiveness of sins, to the extent that they are said to forgive sins and to loose souls. When you hear that this is attributed to them, recognize that it is for your benefit.

"Therefore, let every believer remember that, if he be privately troubled and afflicted with a sense of sins, so that without outside help he is unable to free himself from them, it is part of his duty not to neglect what the Lord has offered to him by way of remedy. Namely, that, for his relief, he should use private confession to his own pastor; and for his solace, he should beg the private help of him whose duty it is, both publicly and privately, to comfort the people of God by the gospel teaching. Hence, it follows that confession of this sort ought to be free so as not to be required of all, but to be commended only to those who know that they have need of it. Then, that those who use it according to their need neither be forced by any rule nor be induced by any trick to recount all their sins. . . .

"Now Christ speaks of the other sort of confession in the Gospel of Matthew: 'If you are offering your gift at the altar, and there remember that your brother has something against you, leave your gift there . . . and go; first be reconciled to your brother, and then come and offer your gift'

(Matt. 5:23-24). For the love, which was broken by our offense, is thus repaired by our acknowledging the wrong we have committed, and asking pardon for it.

"In this class is included the confession of those who have sinned even to the point of offending against the whole church. For if Christ considers the private offense of one man so serious that he bars from the sacred rites all those who sin in any respect against their brothers, until they become reconciled by a just satisfaction, how much greater is the reason that he who offends the church by any evil example should be reconciled to it by acknowledgement of his offense. Thus was the Corinthian received again into communion when he had obediently yielded to correction (II Cor. 2:6).

"This was also the form of confession in the early church as Cyprian also recalls it. He says, 'They do penance for a certain period; then they come to confession, and through the imposition of the hands of bishop and clergy receive the privilege of communion.' Scripture does not know any other manner or form of confession at all, and it is not our task to bind with new bonds consciences that Christ most sternly forbids to enslave . . . .

"The power of the keys has a place in these three kinds of confession: either when the entire church with solemn recognition of its faults implores pardon or when an individual, who has by some notable transgression committed a common offense, declares his repentance, or when one who needs a minister's help on account of a troubled conscience discloses his weakness to him . . . . it is no common or light solace to have present there the ambassador of Christ, armed with the mandate of reconciliation, ... And private absolution is of no less efficacy or benefit, when it is sought by those who need to remove their weakness by a singular remedy. For it often happens that one who hears general promises that are intended for the whole congregation of believers remains nonetheless in some doubt, and as if he had not yet attained forgiveness, still has a troubled mind. Likewise, if he lays open his heart's secret to his pastor, and from his pastor hears that message of the gospel specially directed to himself, 'Your sins are forgiven, take heart' (Matt. 9:2p), he will be reassured in mind and be set free from the anxiety that formerly tormented him." [17]

"Discipline depends for the most part upon the power of the keys and upon spiritual jurisdiction . . . . But because some persons, in their hatred of discipline, recoil from its very name, let them understand this: if no society, indeed, no house which has even a small family, can be kept in proper condition without discipline, it is much more necessary in the church, whose condition should be as ordered as possible . . . .

"The first foundation of discipline is to provide a place for private admonition; that is, if anyone does not perform his duty willingly, or behaves insolently, or does not live honorably, or has committed any act deserving blame—he should allow himself to be admonished; and when the situation demands it, every man should endeavor to admonish his brother. But let pastors and presbyters be especially watchful to do this, for their duty is not only to preach to the people, but to warn and exhort in every house, wherever they are not effective enough in general instruction . . . .

"If anyone either stubbornly rejects such admonitions or shows that he scorns them by persisting in his own vices, after

[17] *Calvin: Institutes of the Christian Religion. The Library of Christian Classics,* Vol. 20. Edited by John T. McNeill, Translated by Ford Lewis Battles. © 1960, W. L. Jenkins. The Westminister Press. By permission.

having been admonished a second time in the presence of witnesses, Christ commands that he be called to the tribunal of the church, that is, the assembly of the elders, and there be more gravely admonished as by public authority, in order that, if he reverences the church, he may submit and obey. If he is not even subdued by this but perseveres in his wickedness, then Christ commands that, as a despiser of the church, he be removed from the believers' fellowship (Matt. 18:15, 17). . . .

"Now, therefore, we begin to see better how the spiritual jurisdiction of the church, which punishes sins according to the Lord's Word, is the best support of health, foundation of order, and bond of unity. . . .

"In such corrections and excommunication, the church has three ends in view. The first is that they who lead a filthy and infamous life may not be called Christians, to the dishonor of God, as if his holy church (cf. Eph. 5:25-26) were a conspiracy of wicked and abandoned men . . . . The second purpose is that the good be not corrupted by the constant company of the wicked, as commonly happens . . . . The third purpose is that those overcome by shame of their baseness begin to repent. They who under gentler treatment would have become more stubborn so profit by the chastisement of their own evil as to be awakened when they feel the rod . . . ." [18]

John Wesley's View
of Confession and Penance

"We grant confession to men to be in many cases of use, public in case of public scandal; private to a

[18] *Ibid.,* Volume 21. Sections quoted from pp. 1229-1233.

spiritual guide for disburthening of the conscience, and as an help to repentance. But to make auricular confession, or particular confession to a priest, necessary to forgiveness and salvation, when God has not so made it, is apparently to teach for doctrine the commandment of men; and to make it necessary in all cases, is to make of what may be a useful means, a dangerous snare, both to the confessor and those that confess." [19]

"The giving of satisfaction to the church in case of scandal, and the imposing of penances upon notorious offenders, is an useful part of ecclesiastical discipline. But to make that a satisfaction to God which is given to the church; and to make our works to satisfy, though but as an appendant to the satisfaction of Christ, we can by no means allow. Not the former, because it is derogatory to the justice of God; not the latter, because it is derogatory to the merits of our Saviour. For what can make a satisfaction to God, but the obedience and suffering of his Son? Or what need is there of another satisfaction after that of our Saviour? Heb. 10:14, 'By one offering he hath perfected for ever, them that are sanctified.' " [20]

JOHN WESLEY'S METHOD OF DEALING
WITH PERSONS GUILTY OF SIN

"They said, 'But we want you likewise to talk with us often, to direct and quicken us in our way, to give us the advices which you well know we need, and to pray with us as well as for us.' I asked, which of you desire this? Let me know your names and places of abode. They did so. But I soon found they were too many for me to talk with severally so

[19] *The Works of The Rev. John Wesley* (16 volumes and index), London: Printed at The Conference-Office, 14, City-Road; by Thomas Cordeux, Agent, 1809-1813. "A Roman Catechism: With a Reply Thereto," Vol. 15, p. 169.
[20] *Ibid.* "A Roman Catechism: With a Reply Thereto," Vol. 15, page 171.

often as they wanted it: so I told them, 'if you will all of you come together, every Thursday, in the evening, I will gladly spend some time with you in prayer, and give you the best advice I can' . . . .

"But as much as we endeavored to watch over each other, we soon found some who did not live the gospel. I do not know that any hypocrites were crept in; for, indeed, there was no temptation: but several grew cold, and gave way to the sins which had long easily beset them: we quickly perceived, there were many ill consequences of suffering these to remain among us; it was dangerous to others, inasmuch as all sin is of an infectious nature; it brought such a scandal on their brethren, as exposed them to what was not properly the reproach of Christ; it laid a stumbling-block in the way of others, and caused the truth to be evil spoken of.

"We groaned under those inconveniences long before a remedy could be found. The people were scattered so wide in all parts of the town, from Wapping to Westminster, that I could not easily see what the behaviour of each person in his own neighbourhood was; so that several disorderly walkers did much hurt before I was apprized of it.

"At length, while we were thinking of quite another thing, we struck upon a method for which we have had cause to bless God ever since. I was talking with several of the society in Bristol concerning the means of paying the debts there, when one stood up and said, 'Let every member of the society give a penny a week till all are paid.' Another answered, 'But many of them are poor, and cannot afford to do it.' 'Then,' said he, 'Put eleven of the poorest with me, and if they can give any thing, well: I will call on them weekly; and, if they can give nothing, I will give for them as well as for myself: and each of you call on eleven of your neighbours

weekly; receive what they give, and make up what is wanting.'
It was done. In awhile some of these informed me, 'they
found such and such a one did not live as he ought.' It struck
me immediately, 'This is the thing, the very thing we have
wanted so long.' I called together all leaders of the classes,
(so we used to term them and their companies), and desired,
that each would make a particular inquiry into the behaviour
of those he saw weekly; they did so: many disorderly walkers
were detected; some turned from the evil of their ways: some
were put away from us: many saw it with fear, and rejoiced
unto God with reverence . . . .

"It is the business of a leader,

   I. To see each person in his class, once a week at the
      least; in order,
        To enquire how their souls prosper;
        To advise, reprove, comfort, or exhort, as occasion
          may require;
        To receive what they are willing to give towards the
          relief of the poor.

  II. To meet the minister and the stewards of the society,
      in order,
        To inform the minister of any that are sick, or of
          any that are disorderly, and will not be reproved.
        To pay to the stewards what they have received of
          their several classes in the week preceding. . . .

"By the blessing of God upon their endeavours to help
one another, many found the pearl of great price . . . .
hence arose such a confidence in each other, that they poured
out their souls into each other's bosom. Indeed they had great
need so to do; for the war was not over, as they had supposed:

but they had to wrestle both with flesh and blood, and with principalities and powers: so that temptations were on every side: and often temptations of such a kind as they knew not how to speak of in class; in which persons of every sort, young and old, men and women, met together . . . .

"In compliance with their desire, I divided them into small companies; putting married or single men, and married and single women together. The chief rules of these Bands (i.e. little companies; so the old English word signifies) run thus:

"In order to confess our faults one to another, and pray one for another, that we may be healed, we intend,

1. To meet once a week, at the least;
2. To come punctually at the hour appointed;
3. To begin with singing or prayer;
4. To speak each of us in order, freely and plainly, the true state of our souls, with the faults we have committed in thought, word, or deed, and the temptations we have felt since our last meeting;
5. To desire some person among us (thence called a leader) to speak his own state first, and then to ask the rest in order, as many and as searching questions as may be, concerning their state, sins, and temptations." [21]

"The Radical Reformation" or the "Gathered" Churches

"The Radical Reformation is as distinctive as Lutheranism, Calvinism, and Anglicanism, and is perhaps

[21] *Ibid.* "A Plain Account of the People Called Methodists in a Letter to The Rev. Mr. Perronet, Vicar of Shoreham, Kent," Volume 6, pp. 280-303. Quotations are from pp. 282, 284, 285, 286, 291, and 292 respectively.

comparably significant in the rise of modern Christianity
. . . . Common to all participants in the Radical Reformation were disappointment in the moral aspects of territorial
Protestantism . . . (all agreed) in freeing church and creed
of what they regarded as the suffocating growth of ecclesiastical tradition and magisterial prerogative." [22]

We deal here with the Anabaptist roots of what Ernst
Troeltsch called the "sect type" as opposed to the "church
type" of religious group. These churches relied heavily on
personal conversion experience as opposed to the sacramental
system and were often characterized by adult baptism.

METHODS OF DEALING WITH SIN THROUGH EXCLUSION FROM AND RESTORATION TO THE COMMUNITY

Ulrich Stadler—1537

"It is proper for the true deacons (of the Word) of the
Lord to have watchful eyes in all this and to judge and treat
everybody in his community according to the mind and Spirit
of Christ, lest that one be bound and not accepted who before
God has been loosed . . . .

"In the matter of exclusion of such (sinners) I hold as
before, namely, that the deacons should exercise the power in
the house of the Lord and with severity punish all who are
disorderly, disobedient, and obstinate and not put up with
them in the house of the Lord, ban them also from the house
of the Lord with the consent of the whole people of God, yea
all sinners who work unrighteousness." [23]

[22] *Spiritual and Anabaptist Writers* (The Library of Christian Classics, Vol. 25), Edited by George Huntston Williams. Published 1957, The West-minister Press. Used by permission.
[23] *Ibid.* "Cherished Instructions on Sin, Excommunication, and the Community of Goods," by Ulrich Stadler, pp. 274-284. Quotation from page 276.

Menno Simons—1550

"*Question 8.* Who, according to Scripture, should be banned or excommunicated? *Answer.* Christ says (Matt. 18:15-17): If thy brother trespass against thee, etc., and will not hear thee or the witnesses, nor the church, let him be unto thee as a heathen man and a publican . . . . In short, all those who openly lead a shameful, carnal life, and those who are corrupted by a heretical, unclean doctrine (Titus 3:10), and who will not be overcome by the wine and oil of the Holy Spirit, but remain, after they have been admonished and sought to be regained in all love and reasonableness, obdurate in their corrupted walk and opinion. They should, at last, in the name of the Lord Jesus Christ, by the power of the Holy Spirit, that is, by the binding Word of God, be reluctantly but unanimously separated from the church of Christ and thereupon, according to the Scriptures, be shunned in all divine obedience, until they repent." [24]

Dietrich Philips—c.1560

"Separation or exclusion must also be practiced for the reason that thereby the offender may be chastised in the flesh and be made ashamed, and so may repent that he may be saved in the day of the Lord Jesus (I Cor. 5:5), which is the highest love, and the very best mastery or medicine for his poor soul, as may be observed in the case of the Corinthian fornicator. Moreover, necessity demands that there be separation from apostates and wicked persons, that the name of God, the gospel of Jesus Christ, and the congregation of the Lord be not on their account put to shame (Ps. 50:21; Ezek. 36:20-24; Rom. 2:24). . . .

[24] *Ibid.* "On the Ban" by Menno Simons, pp. 263-271. Quotation from pp. 270-271.

"And what the congregation of the Lord determines with his Word, the same is judged before God, for Christ gave his congregation the keys of the Kingdom of Heaven (Matt. 16:19) that they might punish, exclude, and put away the wicked, and receive the penitent and believing." [25]

The "Great Awakening" in Colonial America and Revival Meetings in General

Jonathan Edwards—1735

"Persons are first awakened with a sense of their miserable condition by nature, the danger they are in of perishing eternally, and that it is of great importance to them that they speedily escape and get into a better state. Those that before were secure and senseless, are made sensible how much they were in the way to ruin in their former courses. Some are more suddenly seized with convictions . . . their consciences are suddenly smitten, as if their hearts were pierced through with a dart . . . .

"These awakenings, when they have first seized on persons, have had two effects: one was, that they have brought them immediately to quit their sinful practices, and the looser sort have been brought to forsake and dread their former vices and extravagances . . . . And the other effect was, that it put them on earnest application to the means of salvation, reading, prayer, meditation, the ordinances of God's house, and private conferences; their cry was, *What shall we do to be saved?* . . .

"There is a very great variety as to the degree of fear and

[25] *Ibid.* "The Church of God" by Dietrich Philips, pp. 228-260. Quotation from p. 247.

trouble that persons are exercised with before they obtain any comfortable evidences of pardon and acceptance with God: some are from the beginning carried on with abundantly more encouragement and hope than others; some have had ten times less trouble of mind than others . . . . Some have had such a sense of the displeasure of God, and the great danger they were in of damnation, that they could not sleep at night . . . . It has been very common that the deep and fixed concern that has been on person's minds, has had a painful influence on their bodies, and given disturbance to animal nature . . . .

"There is wrought in them a holy repose of soul in God through Christ, and a secret disposition to fear and love him . . . .

"In some, converting light is like a glorious brightness, suddenly shining in upon a person and all around him: they are in a remarkable manner brought *out of darkness into marvellous* light." [26]

THE MID-WEEK PRAYER-MEETING

These were especially common in non-liturgical churches, but also developed in liturgical or sacramental churches through the influence of the pietist movement which spread through Europe and on to America. It was not uncommon to have testimonies and confessions of sins in such group meetings. These meetings were on the local congregational level. Pentecostal and fundamentalistic denominations most commonly continue this practice today.

[26] Jonathan Edwards, *Thoughts on the Revival of Religion in New England, 1740. To Which is Prefixed a Narrative of the Surprising Work of God in Northampton, Mass., 1735.* New York: American Tract Society (no date). Quotes from pp. 28, 29, 30, 47, and 53. For a treatment of the revival movement across the American frontier see: *They Gathered at the River,* by Bernard A. Weisberger. Boston: Little, Brown and Company, 1958.

THE FULTON STREET NOONDAY PRAYER-MEETING

"The Usual Daily Order of Conducting the Meeting":
  Open with singing.
  Read the Scripture.
  Read half the requests (at 12:30 the remainder).
  Prayer.
  Singing.
  Throw the meeting open. (You have fifteen minutes
    of time for the above. Say, brethren, be prompt,
    concise, and keep within the five minutes, in order
    that many may take part.)
  Sing often, read one verse of each hymn you give out.
    If any exceed their time, manifest it by rising.
    Close promptly at one o'clock.
  Benediction.

". . . Each person finds a hymn-book in his seat; all sing
with heart and voice . . . . Meantime requests in sealed
envelopes have been going up to the desk for prayer. Every
nook and corner is filled—the doorways and stairways—and
the upper room is now filled, and we hear the voice of singing.

"A deep, solemn silence settles down upon our meeting. It
is holy ground. The leader stands with slips of paper in his
hand . . . .

"All is now breathless attention. A tender solicitude
spreads over all those upturned faces.

"The chairman reads, 'A son in North Carolina desires the
fervent, effectual prayers of the righteous of this congregation
for the immediate conversion of his mother in Connecticut.'

"In an instant a father rises, "I wish to ask the prayers of
this meeting for two sons and a daughter.'

"And he sits down and bursts into tears, and lays his head

down on the railing of the seat before him, and sobs like a broken-hearted child. We say in our heart, 'Oh heart-stricken parent! do you not know that these children are close by the kingdom!

"A brother rises and pours out his heart in prayer for 'that mother,' for those 'two sons' and 'that daughter' . . . .

"Another, 'Prayers are requested of the people of God for a young man, once a professor of religion, but now a wanderer, and going astray. These Christian parents invoke a continued interest in your prayers' . . . .

"Then there arose a sailor, now one no more, by reason of ill-health, but daily laboring for sailors. He was converted on board a man-of-war, and he knew how hard it was for the converted sailor to stand up firm against the storm of jeers and reproaches, and taunts of a ship's crew. 'Now I am here,' he said, 'to represent one who has requested me to ask your prayers for a converted sailor, this day gone to sea. I parted from him a little time ago, and his fear is that he may dishonor the cause of the blessed Redeemer. Will you pray for this sailor?'

Prayer was offered for his keeping and guidance.

Then came the closing hymn, the benediction, and the parting for twenty-four hours." [27]

[27] Lewis O. Thompson, *How To Conduct Prayer-Meetings*, Boston: D. Lothrop and Company 1880. Passages quoted from pp. 290, 292, 293, 295, 296.

6

WHAT IS BEING
DONE BY THE CHURCHES?

A psychiatrist was speaking to a group of ministers from a small fundamentalist denomination and complimented them on being "fifty years behind the times in their psychology." They had been spared the long Freudian detour which the more progressive denominations had made in their attempt to keep abreast of the times. Psychological and sociological fads may resemble women's fashions in one respect; even if a woman does not change at all she will be in style periodically. The implied question of this chapter and the previous one seen together is: Maybe the churches have had valuable healing resources which they are presently giving up in favor of "modern psychology."

The most comprehensive study of mental health to date

is the ten-volume opus written by the Joint Commission on
Mental Illness and Health. In the *Community Resources in
Mental Health,* the commission states what the role of the
churches should be in fostering mental health, and it is quite
different from the statements (see Chapter 5) of seven denominations indicating the resources they believe they have in
dealing with alienated and distressed people.

> The church can be related to the field of mental health at
> two levels—in a promotional role and in a supportive role.
> Through its recreational, social, and family-education pro-
> grams, the church helps to promote and maintain mental
> health; through the offices of the clergy, it functions in the
> supportive role. . . .
>   1. The clergy can provide spiritual support to emotion-
> ally disturbed people in times of stress and crisis.
>   2. The clergy can counsel on religious matters, applying
> all the psychological insight at their disposal.
>   3. The clergy can "listen" and identify cases with prob-
> lems outside the religious framework, and refer them to
> proper community resources.
>   4. Clergymen with psychological insight but with little or
> no training in pastoral counseling perhaps may counsel on
> personal or interpersonal problems with little emotional con-
> tent. The difficulty comes in recognizing the complexity of
> the problems.
>   5. Only clergymen with intensive training in clinical prac-
> tice under expert supervision should ever attempt to counsel
> persons with mental and emotional problems. In the majority
> of cases, clergymen should probably confine themselves to
> playing the first three roles, and seek help from the secular
> mental health resources on problems requiring a higher level
> of competency.[1]

[1] Robinson, Reginald, David F. DeMarche and Mildred K. Wagle, *Community Resources in Mental Health,* New York: Basic Books, Inc., Publishers,
1960, pp. 248-249.

Such a position is obviously contradictory to the assumption of the churches, according to their statements, that their sacraments, rites, and methods go right to the heart of the problem of *guilt,* which is so central in mental illness. They hold redemption to be radically therapeutic and not peripherally "supportive." At least that is what they *say.*

A Survey of Current Thinking and Practice Concerning Guilt

The denominations chosen represent a broad spectrum of historic traditions and practices, varying degrees of acculturation to the American scene, different types of hierarchical authority and ecclesiastical organization, and differences in theological or doctrinal outlook. This survey makes no pretensions at great statistical sophistication. It is rather an exploratory study. For example, among the large family of Eastern Orthodox churches, the Russian, Roumanian, or Greek churches might just as well have been chosen as the Syrian Antiochian Orthodox Archdiocese of New York and North America, which was used. Roman Catholic priests were selected at random from *The Official Catholic Directory,* 1961. The Anglican tradition is represented by priests from the Protestant Episcopal Church annual directory. Lutherans were drawn at random from the 1962 Yearbook of the United Lutheran Church in America. The current list of The United Presbyterian Church in the United States of America was used. The Methodist Church presented somewhat of a problem because 8 questionnaires were returned to the sender by the Post Office (perhaps accounted for by the frequent movement within this group).

And, again arbitrarily, among several Baptist churches that
could have been used, the Southern Baptist Convention list
was used. Again let it be emphasized that the writer is aware
of the enormous number of variables in such a random sample—50 each from 7 denominations, or a total of 350. The
fact that 105 completed the questionnaire indicates the keen
interest in the subject. Many wrote extensive letters.

In order to help the reader get a "feel" for the survey,
both the individually typed letter and the questionnaire are
reproduced just as they were received by the responding
clergymen (see Figures 1 and 2).

Rather than to present the summary of the findings in
the form of statistical tables, a general running commentary
on trends and their implications will be used. The number
of replies is too small in any one group to be statistically significant: Orthodox, 17; Roman Catholic, 9; Episcopal, 23;
Lutheran, 16; Presbyterian, 20; Methodist, 12, and Baptist,
8. No second mailing or follow-up was used.

1. *Authenticity of the statements* is generally accepted by
81% of the clergymen replying. There seems to be confusion
among the Protestant ministers as to whether their church
takes a certain position on confession or church discipline,
many of them qualifying their answers by saying that whereas
it may be their historic tradition it is no longer the practice.
Episcopalians tended to go into some detail on whether or
not the Book of Common Prayer and the Articles of Religion
were authoritative for today's church practices. Both Episcopalians and Lutherans wanted to list the General Confession,
which is part of the preparation in the liturgy for Holy Communion. One described those "who go through the act of
Public Confession prior to Communion." Perhaps he had
tongue in cheek when he used the term "act" since he later

University of Illinois | Department of Psychology
URBANA, ILLINOIS

1005 West Nevada
Urbana, Illinois
March 30, 1962

The Rev. John R. Doe
Holy Trinity Church
Richfield, Ohio

Dear Pastor Doe:

I am one of three professors of Pastoral Theology doing research at the University of Illinois. We are concerned with the genesis, function, and resolution of personal guilt.

Seven denominations are included in this study. You are one of fifty ministers representing your church, and your answer will help provide a fair sampling of your denomination.

If you will kindly assist me by answering the enclosed few questions, I shall gladly send you a summary of the findings.

Naturally, it is impossible to give a complete description of all the teachings and practices of your denomination concerning sin and guilt, confession and forgiveness, church discipline and pastoral guidance in the restoration of the sinner. An attempt has been made to cite authentic, typical, and where possible, authoritative statements from the founders or leaders and significant documents of your denomination.

Of course, your answers are confidential. Feel free to use the reverse side of the questionnaire for further comments, examples, or issues you feel are pertinent.

Appreciative of your concern and help, I remain

Fraternally yours,

David Belgum

The Rev. David Belgum, Ph.D.

P. S. Please use the enclosed AIR MAIL self-addressed envelope for your reply.

FIGURE 1. A LETTER TO PASTORS.

1. Does the enclosed statement represent the authentic teaching and practice of your denomination?   Yes _____ ,   No _____

    If not, why not?

2. If your answer to question 1 is yes (or yes with qualifications), how frequently do you use the methods, rites, or procedures as indicated in the enclosed statement?

3. How many different persons have utilized the methods, rites, or procedures as indicated on the enclosed statement in the past twelve months? _____

4. How many adult (or confirmed) members belong to your church?_____

5. How do you judge or evaluate the effectiveness of these methods in dealing with persons suffering from guilt?

6. With what sorts of persons suffering from guilt have you found these methods to be ineffective (not providing an adequate solution)?

    Why not?   What reasons or factors account for the failure?

7. Do you regard these methods or procedures as psychologically therapeutic as regards mental health and personal adjustment or only theologically (or sacramentally) pertinent?

    Please Explain.

8. In ministering to a person suffering from guilt, what determines whether you use one or another of the following methods:

    a.   The methods or procedures indicated on the enclosed statement?

    b.   Make referral to a psychiatrist or other psychotherapist?

    c.   Other methods you may wish to indicate?

(You may use other side.)

FIGURE 2. PASTOR'S QUESTIONNAIRE.

says, "that Public Confession does not mean very much and is thus not very effective." A Methodist made this comment:

> "Some are practising the endeavor found in the statement, others are not . . . but perhaps we have risen above the motive of the fundamental Gospel with 74% of our church white-collar workers. Many of our people are social status-seekers. Anyone complying with the normal Gospel would be called a fanatic."

Others spoke nostalgically as though the statement were valid enough but that "times have changed."

Among Episcopal, Lutheran, and Presbyterian ministers where there was almost an equal division between the outright "yes" and "no" answers, there seems to be need for clarification. It must be confusing for parishioners who move from one parish to another and do not know what resources are actually available. One respondent said, "We don't go to that much 'trouble.'" Another reported that in the Methodist church the endeavors found in the statement were not practiced with any consistency ". . . but there is much talk as to its authenticity" (perhaps because of the current emphasis on a group therapy not unlike Wesley's Class method). A minister writes, "patterns and times have changed. Drift rather than detailed rejection is the record."

2. *Frequency of use* is obviously influenced by the official stand of the denomination. The Eastern Orthodox and Roman Catholic churches require that a member in good standing must go to Confession and receive the Sacrament of Holy Communion at least once a year. Such emphasis ranges from weekly confessions in a Roman Catholic parish to churches that offer the opportunity for confession four times a year,

to others who make it available "upon request" leaving the initiative entirely up to the penitent. In those churches practicing specific forms of church discipline for (unrepented) sin and guilt, the procedure is used only when a specific case is brought before the "Session" or congregation.

A Methodist minister indicated that such Wesleyan methods were used "rarely—the church has grown too soft for these methods. We might be better off if these methods were reinstated." A Baptist preacher sent along a copy of an amendment to his congregation's constitution, in which the notion of excommunication reminiscent of Menno Simons' admonition to the early Anabaptists is reinstated (see page 90):

> B. Should a member become an offense to the church and to its good name by reason of immoral or unchristian conduct, the deacons will appoint a committee of two deacons who with the pastor shall investigate the offense and make a faithful effort to get the offending member to repent and amend his ways. If their effort fails, then they will bring all the facts regarding the offense to the deacons for their consideration and if in their judgment the facts require church discipline, then they will present all the facts to the church.

There appeared to be a feeling among many that these methods of their various denominations, where dropped, should be reinstated.

3. *How many different persons have used these methods?* Two Catholic priests simply said "thousands" during the past year. Among churches where such private confession is optional (An Episcopal priest said, "All may; some should; none must."), or where church discipline of some sort is available, there was a total of 76 clergymen. There were 38

ministers who said no one had used these methods in the past year. Of these, 21 believed the methods indicated were authentic for their denomination; 17 believed they were not. What can account for the fact that about as many who do believe in these methods as who do not believe in their authenticity neglected to use them? Could it be a confusion of the problem? As one pastor said, "People come to me with problems, marital friction, etc., rarely with a straight sense of personal guilt to confess."

An equal number (38) of the 76 ministers had used the methods of their various churches from a few times to as many as 100 times in the past year. Although it is hard to weed out those who might have included contemporary counseling in this category, evidently a large active proportion of the clergy still deal in these traditional terms. When some ask, what is the church doing about mental illness due to unresolved guilt, perhaps the answer is, quite a lot. Nevertheless, 50 per cent utilization is hardly sufficient. And perhaps the fact that many ministers (like the one quoted above) do not see "guilt" as the big problem, helps to account for the many who do not use the indigenous, unique, and most direct methods for dealing with personal guilt.

4. *The question of the size of the church* does not appear to be pertinent and will not be discussed. Statistical investigation would call logically for regional categories, urban-rural separation, etc., but such analysis is beyond the scope of this study.

5. *How do you evaluate the effectiveness of these methods?* Many clergymen feel that our age is not amenable to the classic therapy for guilt. A Lutheran pastor summed up the thinking of several in this group:

I would question the general value of a formal office of absolution for the purpose of nurturing contrition and faith on
the basis of fear and "terrors of conscience." There are two
reasons. Our age of popular psychological knowledge and
freedom no longer sees many fear-stricken consciences. Secondly, there is no longer much heeding, in Protestant circles,
at least, of any formal authoritarianism in spiritual matters.
I believe very much in the power of the Keys, but the method
of the administration apparently must be revised with history. At the same time I realize the subtle danger of failure
in communicating both the Will and Grace of God. When
this happens, the result is that real spiritual guilt is replaced
by a secular and pragmatic distress at personal tragedy or
failure. I doubt if the kind of guilt Luther speaks of really
exists today. Furthermore, I doubt if we can, or should, attempt to produce such a guilt in order then to absolve it.

The writer read this response to the questionnaire after
having returned from a routine visit to Galesburg State Research Hospital, where two other seminary professors and
Dr. O. Hobart Mowrer were currently conducting therapy
with a group of psychotic women. One doubts whether the
dread, despair, or *Anfechtung* of which Luther wrote could
possibly have been any more complete. For several patients
the suffering, alienation, and hopelessness seemed *total* indeed! There was no need to "produce such a guilt"; it was
already there in abundance.

The clergymen actually using these methods are closest
to what psychologists would call the "clinical situation."
What ingredients do they find present in the situation when
these procedures work effectively? (Forty-six judged them "effective.")

(a) *Faith* is considered an essential prerequisite for the
treatment of guilt, and, although not largest in number,

seemed to be an underlying assumption, a qualitative factor. Presumably a penitent's belief or trust in the efficacy of the church's ministry is crucial here. A Roman Catholic priest writes:

> Such an *instructed* Catholic knows that God is not One who will "forgive, but not forget"—he knows that when the words of absolution have been spoken, the sin is forgiven, he is restored to the friendship of God, so why any recriminations? Why any sense of guilt? Of course, where restitution is involved, it must be made insofar as the individual is capable. Only in this particular case might a sense of guilt persist.

(b) *Sincerity of repentance* is another precondition to effectiveness. The motivation must be genuine and appropriate. The person who makes light of his guilt, continues to rationalize himself out of responsibility for his predicament, or who retains a desire for his former "pleasures" is not going to get much benefit from the ministrations of the church, according to the ministers who have had the most experience with such cases. Someone has said, "He who finds pleasure in vice and pain in virtue is inexperienced in both."

(c) *Sharing the guilt* and burden is essential to the effectiveness of these methods. A Presbyterian minister replied, "It is most therapeutic and cleansing for the soul not only to admit one's guilt, but to have another accepting person nearby to enter into the burden of your guilt." An Orthodox priest writes, "This sort of format affords a natural outlet for guilt and associated emotions. Since it is a face to face contact, serious problems can be followed up by the priest." This assumes an on-going concern for, not a superficial institutional interest in, the burden in order that it may be dealt with adequately. A Methodist preacher says, "I judge the group and individual sharing and confession to be very effective when we take time to try this, but I think most Methodists have no idea of what these could mean to them."

It appears that the *willingness to share* is an important criterion in determining effectiveness; it is opposed to the desire to remain isolated and alienated from community.

(d) *A changed life* (cited 17 times) was the most frequently stated criterion. Ministers are quite realistic and pragmatic in this regard. This criterion can best be used in the smaller congregation where the clergyman knows his congregation intimately. One clergyman said he knew his people so well that he could distinguish between those with serious problems who had not yet resolved them and those who were restored to constructive, healthful living. A priest said it was sometimes possible to sense the relief of nervous tension during the confessional itself. Other symptoms of problem behavior that had been concretely changed were hatred, jealousy, and extra-marital relations. It helps to "establish mental stability" according to one respondent. A Methodist says, "In some cases I believe that it has brought what, over a period of time, would seem to be lasting results, *new life.*" A Roman Catholic priest wrote that it is possible to judge the effectiveness of his ministrations (penance) "From the frequency of his falling repeatedly into the same sin or from his correction of his faults." Another priest listed three criteria for evaluation: "(1) The frequency of relapse, (2) What is the person doing by way of 'breaking' the sin, and (3) Relief of anxiety." Perhaps these various replies may be summed up by the Scripture passage, "Ye shall know them by their fruits." It is the criterion referred to in Chapter 2 as "satisfaction," which others may call "growth in grace" or "Amendment of life."

Another way to get at the same factor is to ask the question about effectiveness in the negative, which was done in the next item on the questionnaire.

6. *With ·what kinds of persons and for what reasons are these methods ineffective?* What accounts for the failure to transform lives which is so often leveled at the churches? A Roman Catholic priest answered the question in this way:

> The insincere—those who really are not in earnest about breaking a habit of sin. The uneducated who consider the powers of the confessional as magical. A "bad confession." They are either so attached to the pleasures or advantages deriving from the sin that they do not really intend to stop the sin or the habit, or they are presumptuous of God's help, thinking God will change them without their effort or co-operation.

(a) *Psychological problems* and unconscious dynamics are assumed to make the methods of the various denominations ineffective. There were 36 references to "pathological guilt," obsessive-compulsive habits, mental illness, "abnormal scrupulosity," and other symptoms of psychopathology. These are considered to lie beyond the reach of sacramental or other religious ministrations, and to lie within the field of the psychiatrist. Here is a typical "chicken-or-the-egg, which-came-first?" problem. Are these people unable to benefit from confession because they are mentally ill, or are they still mentally ill because they have not gone through the classic "therapy" of repentance-confession-satisfaction?

At this point Mowrer (*The Crisis in Psychiatry and Re-*

ligion) would chide the clergy for selling themselves short and passing the moral buck to psychiatry. And he would be especially agitated by the minister who replied, " 'Guilt' to me is a psychiatric term . . . . I try always to refer 'guilt' cases to a competent psychiatrist." The minister called this a "matter of semantics," and said, " 'Sense of sin' is chiefly what I deal with. Confession is very helpful." But there seems to be more than semantics involved here. (See Chapter 4, Patient or Penitent?) The crucial question is: Can the church deal redemptively with deeply repressed guilt of long duration, or is the church limited to dealing with *fresh* guilt? The same ministers who would refer "guilt cases" no doubt preach and teach that the church has the answer to the problem of guilt caused by sin.

An older priest of the Episcopal Church counterbalances the view of the minister cited above. He says:

> I am tempted to say, (it is ineffective) with psychotics and emotionally disturbed people. But continued pastoral counseling and repetitions of Penance can have therapeutic effect in this area of guilt. Again I say that I have seen this happen over a period of thirty-two years in the ministry. My experience is admittedly limited but it does not permit me to say that the procedure is "ineffective."

A Methodist minister believes that the Freudian interpretation of behavior has invalidated Wesley's class-method approach, which he labels as "ineffective." He feels that "The approach is superficial, supposes all motivation is conscious, all wrongdoing is under conscious control." This raises the question of responsibility for "sin" or "wrongdoing" and goes back to the "sin-or-sickness" controversy discussed previously.

(b) *Hardness of heart,* to use a Scriptural phrase, describes the reason for ineffectiveness, in the minds of 43 respondents. This group may be subdivided into three classes: unbelief, insincerity, and unwillingness to change. These three are the reverse side of the coins listed under the question of what makes these methods *effective.* An added comment may be in order. These are the guilty persons who talk a lot but do little. They profess to desire help but lack sincere motivation.

A pastor cites the case of a woman who had been depressed and incapacitated concerning her normal familial responsibilities. Life held out no joy or rewards; she was decompensated. She had talked much about her misery to various ministers and counselors, including a series of sessions at the local mental health clinic, for a year-and-a-half, but she had lacked a sincere desire to amend her life. In fact, while she was talking to the psychotherapist at the clinic, she was having an affair with a neighbor. The pastor asked if she was not deriving some sexual satisfaction out of talking about these intimate relationships (her adolescent fornication and later sexual experiences). She acknowledged that she was and faced openly the central question—Did she still cherish the past way of life in spite of what it had cost her (loss of joy with her husband and children)? She made a decision, confessed all to her husband, and returned to receive absolution in the church. Her husband commented on how spontaneous smiles had replaced the gloom, on the vital relationship they now had, and on the simple fact that for a solid week she had gotten up and made breakfast for the family— evidently a drastic reform in and of itself.

The reason for citing this case at this point is to highlight what many clergymen reported, namely: that without genuine motivation *and* willingness to make amendment of life, any confession is patently invalid. This woman had "gone through the Order for Public Confession" and received Communion "unworthily" dozens of times, but because she was ill-prepared she had found no "balm of Gilead," no healing. Psychotherapy could not help either. There seems to be no cure for those with "hardness of heart."

(c) *Lack of a loving group* was listed by 7 ministers as a serious handicap in the recovery of the guilt-ridden. The church is supposed to be the "beloved community," the "redemptive fellowship." A Methodist minister writes:

> A group of like-minded or compassionate persons is needed for constructive growth; or else a church more intent upon personal spiritual renewal and rebirth, in order to give a (repentant) person a context in which to express the new life.

Not only has "church discipline" been long-neglected according to several, but, if it were practiced, it would probably not convey the intended redemptive and restorative purpose of loving concern, but rather a harsh and pharisaical punishment and rejection.

No doubt any minister would be glad for the resource of one parish in which the priest describes how laymen can be used:

> Occasionally a problem which gives rise to this (deeper) kind of guilt can be dealt with by one or more laymen who have previously experienced a similar situation. In such a case the persons are then brought together for the purpose of understanding a problem and thus be able to deal with the

guilt or find meaning in the normal Confession-Absolution experiences of the Church.

This is the "elder brother" approach that has been found so effective in Alcoholics Anonymous, which in turn borrowed heavily from the Oxford Group and its experimentally-minded minister-leader, Frank Buchman. There is no reason why this "bearing-one-another's-burdens" resource should have to be so *novel* since it was taken quite for granted in New Testament churches. Indeed, it is indigenous to the effective cure of souls.

7. *Are these methods psychologically therapeutic or only theologically pertinent?* As may be expected, a large majority (75) said unequivocally that the methods available in their churches for dealing with guilt were psychologically therapeutic as well as theologically pertinent. Thirteen evaded the issue by not answering the question. Twelve had serious doubts about their therapeutic value, felt they were harmful, or, at best, of uncertain and unpredictable value.

When asked to explain further, many stressed the fact that man is a unit, a whole being. It is a false dichotomy to try to divide him up into theological, psychological, social, economic, etc., parts, like so many pieces of a pie. As one said, "A person brings his whole life for forgiveness, therefore absolution should affect mental health and personal adjustment; if it is *only* 'theologically pertinent,' this is a rather sterile theology." An Orthodox priest replied:

> We can tell that this method has a definite psychological therapy. The participant feels and knows that his sins are forgiven. They react as new people who are born again. They are reconciled with God and neighbor by using this new way of coping with daily problems.

Another minister says, "Decidedly psychologically therapeutic. It must take in the *whole* man: body, soul, mind, emotions, imagination, reason, aspirations, etc., etc."

An Episcopal priest refused to be drawn into the questionnaire's admittedly artificial dichotomy:

> This distinction seems very strange. When God works sacramentally, He works in and through the physical world—the common and ordinary things with which we are in contact, and this certainly includes psychological ends accomplished by word and action. Our Lord's actions were psychologically therapeutic in many cases and also theological (dealing with the relationship with God).

Another pastor continues this line of thought:

> In Confession we are dealing with the whole man—mind, body and soul. Psychosomatic illness which can be traced to hatreds and resentments have been greatly helped in the confessional. I do not see how we could say that we are dealing only with the soul in any instance.

A clergyman replying by letter said:

> Private confession is helpful in many instances. . . . My experience indicates that the methods under discussion are psychologically and therapeutically helpful as well as theologically and sacramentally. I have counselled successfully as priest when trained psychiatrists have failed. It is amazing how some problems respond to the "therapy of grace" which the church provides when other methods fail. The fact of God has tremendous psychological impact.

Many ministers who believe the methods for treating the guilt-ridden person are effective both psychologically *and* theologically raise a note of caution. All it takes to invalidate these methods is to put the cart before the horse, to do the right thing for the wrong reason, to prostitute religion to hedonistic ends. How might this happen? Two Lutheran pastors replied as follows:

> Psychologically therapeutic; but when "peace of mind" is concerned, "sound theology" is pushed into the background. Both psychologically therapeutic and theologically pertinent. But again, I hope your inquiry is searching for more than a ready-made cure-all for the "burdened and heavy laden" (guilty). Jesus was more than a psychologist.

A Roman Catholic priest stresses the need for keeping first things first in the following words:

> First of all healing insofar as God is concerned—the removal of guilt is infallibly efficacious where there is real sorrow because of a supernatural motive and a sincere intention of amendment. Serenity and peace of mind frequently follow upon a good confession.

Perhaps those who would agree with the latter type of response have in mind the words of Jesus that one should seek first the Kingdom of God and His righteousness and then all these other things will be added unto him. Such thinking places *reconciliation* foremost and any wholesome improvement in mental health and personal adjustment as secondary gains—God-pleasing and wonderful, but nevertheless only a consequence and never a primary goal. A Christian should never have a hedonistic search for pleasure and health as his ultimate or highest good.

Much unnecessary name-calling and argument over the "peace of mind" fad could have been avoided if this simple principle of putting first things first had been observed. There would also be no need to throw out the baby with the bath water.

8. *What determines whether you (a) use the methods indicated on the statement, (b) make referral to a psychotherapist, or (c) use other methods?* Here was an attempt to make the clergyman filling out the questionnaire face again the issue of the effectiveness of the methods his church says are available for dealing with personal guilt.

The vast majority of responses cited clear or advanced *psychopathology* as the criterion for assuming that the minister needed to turn to psychiatry or some other form of secular psychotherapy. This was indicated by such terms as "abnormal behavior," "mental illness," "severity of mental symptoms," "insurmountable mental block," "psychotic or neurotic," "when so mentally disturbed he cannot follow the procedures of the church rationally," and "when guilt feelings are rooted deep in the sub-conscious."

Such cases were considered to be beyond the competence of the minister. The questionnaire should perhaps have been more refined at this point in order to distinguish among the various alternatives available for specific kinds of behavior. With certain types of behavior (suicide attempts, exhibitionism, and other forms of bizarre "acting out" behavior) there is no choice but to do what the law requires. What is of more crucial interest to the clergy are the cases for which there is a live option, such as the woman cited above who had gone to the mental health clinic for a year-and-a-half, but whose condition was not serious enough to require hospitalization.

It is surprising that more ministers did not mention the custodial facilities over which the psychotherapist with an M.D. degree (the psychiatrist) alone has the "office of the keys," for any counselor comes across those troubled, perplexed persons who leave the office with the unresolved question still hanging in the air, "What if he does something violent before our next appointment?" The minister does not have the protective custody of a mental ward with its round-the-clock staff of attendants and nurses as part of his resources. Yet no clergymen referred to the protective environment of a mental hospital as the reason for seeking psychiatric aid. Perhaps it was in the back of their minds.

If the reason for referral to psychiatry is the notion that all mental illness must of necessity be treated by a medical man since it is indeed a *sickness,* rather than a distorted way of life, the question of Chaptar 4 (Patient or Penitent?) must again be raised.

Psychopathology is a term made up of three Greek roots and means literally "the *study* of the *suffering* of the *soul.*" If the "pathos" of the "psyche" is deepest when involved in incapacitating guilt, such suffering should be a major concern of the church.

The methods used by clergymen which were not listed in the statements mailed to them included: pastoral counseling in 14 cases, other forms of secular counseling, social service agencies (especially those for marital discord), Alcoholics Anonymous, prayer and worship, and social activities within the church's program which are designed to strengthen fellowship and interpersonal relationships. One minister said that the resource of Confession in a formal sense must be seen in the larger context of total pastoral care. It could not be used in isolation, e.g., dissociated from Christian faith and worship, nor from other aspects of Christian life, such as a man's vocation and the stewardship of his life.

Conclusion: A Clear Need for a Revitalized Ministry

This questionnaire has revealed confusion among many of the clergy. They do not agree on what resources are authentic and available within their own denominations, for effective ministry to alienated, guilt-ridden people. They are not always certain about the nature of guilt nor its resolution. Not many would be as outspoken as the minister most pessimistic about referral:

> If the clergyman, to the best of his knowledge, believes that an individual is suffering from a morbid guilt, he could well refer to a psychiatrist, and unfortunately usually does. I say unfortunately because from my personal observation, for all the good that psychiatrists do, the individual might well save his money and see his minister on a regular basis. The only commodity which one would think the psychiatrist would have the most regard for, "time," is the one commodity on which they are short. Thorazine—EST (electroshock therapy)—insulin—etc. The a-theoretical basis on which so many of them work would make me extremely cautious in referring to psychiatrists. The minister, of course, is not equipped to handle organic complaints and if such is even suspected should immediately be referred to a physician. However, barring an organic condition, there doesn't seem to be any area which a minister cannot safely delve into with a parishioner.

And so we see the controversial nature of this entire question.

We have heard from many clergymen who represent many parts of the country and a variety of traditions. Except for occasional interpretive comment, the ministers and priests have been allowed to speak for themselves in this survey.

The question that now confronts us is: Where do we go from here? How can the powerful and health-giving resources to which so many have testified be made more generally available in the churches? How can the ministers make more effective use of the healing resources which lie unused within their own denominational traditions? How can the members of the churches take seriously and practically what is theoretically preached from the pulpits and written in doctrinal textbooks? How can old measures be relevant for our time?

These are some of the questions which will be dealt with in the final chapter.

7

A FUNCTIONAL
CONFESSIONAL

*When the unclean spirit has gone out
of a man, he passes through waterless
places seeking rest; and finding none he
says, "I will return to my house from
which I came." And when he comes he
finds it swept and put in order. Then he
goes and brings seven other spirits more
evil than himself, and they enter and dwell
there; and the last state of that man becomes worse than the first. (Luke 11:24-26)*

Jesus said that if someone asks you for bread it would be
unthinkable to give him a stone. When persons suffering
from the many painful and debilitating consequences of
personal guilt come to the church for healing they must be
taken seriously and treated effectively. If the church cannot
minister functionally at this point, there is little point in a
big "turn-out" Sunday morning for casual worship.

The treatment of the theme so far has been critical, his-
torical, or developmental. This chapter will be constructive
and attempt to propose a workable pastoral-care approach to
the problem of sin and guilt which will combine the insights
from tradition, the experience of contemporary clergy, and

118

certain counseling methods. Among other methods, "vocational rehabilitation" holds some promise as a pastoral-care model in preference to the classical forms of psychotherapy and will be discussed in detail later.

Essential Elements in a Functional Confessional

There are three elements or factors which drive a person into the agony of guilt and work to keep him there. These are: *sins* of various sorts; *pride*, or hardness of heart, which prevents him from fully realizing his predicament; and *hypocrisy*, which is his non-functional attempt to deal with the guilt and social alienation caused by his sins. Figure 3 shows how these three surround the Ego to keep the person within a narrow circle of egocentric isolation.

The gracious invitation the church gives the individual is to exchange pride and hardness of heart for *repentance*, and to acknowledge that his wrongful deeds and life are contrary to God's will, or *judgment*, as well as an offense to society, which he has betrayed by not playing the game according to the rules. Instead of fighting this judgment with rationalizations and defense mechanisms, he should repent and desire a new way of life. But the church does not leave the individual floundering in generalizations. The second part of the invitation is that the guilty person forsake hypocrisy and practice *confession* and openness toward others, toward God and toward persons whom he has offended or deceived by the lies of hypocritical pretense. As a result, condemnation is replaced by *forgiveness*. God *and* society view this changed person in a new light. He is now free from the fear of discovery and the paralysis of judgment, and is able

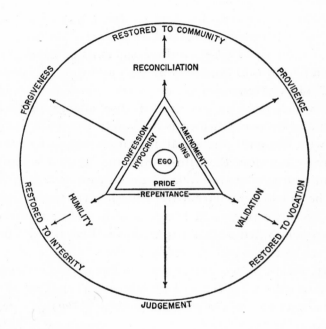

FIGURE 3. ESSENTIAL ELEMENTS IN A FUNCTIONAL CONFESSIONAL.

to expend the energy he formerly directed toward his sins toward a constructive *amendment* of life. Just as sins are contrary to God's *providence,* or plan for nature and the social order, so amended lives seek to co-operate with God's created order. (For example, many sins of concupiscence are against man's nature.)

Notice that each of the three "prescriptions" of the church operate in dynamic relationship to each other and lead to restoration, to *integrity* concerning ultimate destiny, to *community* with fellowmen, and to *vocation* in the expenditure of energies in some mission of service.

It takes *humility* to view one's life with integrity, to see oneself objectively and truthfully, neither with a morbid sense of inferiority nor with a boastful arrogance. But humility is not generated out of thin air. It is the by-product of a correct inner attitude of repentance *and* open social interaction with others through confession, whereby a person gets what some have called "consensual validation." This is how a person gets an accurate estimate of his life and how he is restored to personal integrity.

In slang terms, someone will challenge the person who is a big talker, the verbal exhibitionist, by saying bluntly, "Put up or shut up!" Some people are long on talk but short on action. "He talks big, but you can't count on him." Such persons are not well accepted by society. On the contrary, those ministers in the survey (see pages 106 f.) who felt the confessional was effective, cited "a changed life" most frequently. The combination of honest confession *and* amendment of life makes *reconciliation* possible. Scripture speaks of joy and singing among the angels over one such person's restoration. And even popular newspaper and magazine articles speak in glowing terms about the rehabilitated prisoner, the recovered alcoholic, the person who has openly "turned over a new leaf." Such persons are in a very real sense "restored to community." And it is a rewarding, abundant life compared with the egocentric isolation formerly experienced as a result of rebellious sinning and secretive hypocrisy.

In a sense we have come full circle, for the amendment of life is linked with repentance in the acid test of what one does with this "new lease on life." The Church has been right in saying that the penitent who has mental reservations about giving up his sins, who thinks he can eat his cake and have it too, has thereby made the entire process invalid. Just as it is sacramentally invalid, so it is also psychologically ineffective and non-therapeutic. It is said in Scripture that those who eat and drink unworthily at the Lord's Supper do so to their own damnation, which doesn't consist in simply not being rescued from their guilt, but being confirmed in it. The solid merger of the amendment of life *and* repentance provides a *validation* of the person's intention and goal, namely: making a functional confession. In Paul's phrase, he is not just "beating the air."

Someone may ask, "Why is it that you are concerned about restoration to everyone but God? The penitent's relationship to the community, to his own integrity, and to his mission are fine; but what about his relationship to God?" The answer is that all of this relates to God and man's eternal destiny. This is the theological dimension discussed in Chapter 2. To portray the relationship of the functional confessional to God would require a third dimension, height. The circle in Figure 3 would be the bottom of a cone with the various factors or elements of the circle flowing upward toward the apex of the cone, that point at which all would meet; for none of these factors is separate from God's involvement in his created order, least of all the person himself, who is created in the very Image of God. Nor is God disinterested either in the catastrophe of guilt or the joyful rescue and salvation of any of his children.

Another will ask, "But how does Jesus Christ fit into the picture?" Indeed! The *Christ*ian Church is not simply *named* after Christ; it is his very Body here on earth. The mission and work of Christ are an inseparable part of the whole invitation of the Church to the sinner to use the confessional "for Christ's sake." The Church has produced more writing and doctrine on this subject than, perhaps, on any other phase of the Christian religion. The invitation of the church at this point may be called gracious (see page 119) precisely because of the *Grace* of Christ. Grace implies that a gift is being given or extended. It is unearned and does not originate within the recipient. That is why in Figure 3, the three "prescriptions" are outside the triangle while the "problems" originate with the sinner. A detailed discussion of the basis for this holy activity in the doctrines of incarnation, atonement, resurrection, etc., is beyond the scope of this presentation. These are here assumed as "givens" in the historic Christian tradition.

A major concern must be not to short-circuit or shortcut any of the steps or essential elements in the treatment of the guilty person, for any easing up or cutting of corners drastically weakens the church's effectiveness.

Judgment is often withheld as a "kindness" to someone. An attorney lives in adultery but continues to teach a Sunday School class. On the side he is also violating the housing inspection code with several of his rental properties. A dentist is convicted of performing illegal abortions, but his case is hushed up down at the court house and he continues to be one of the most "respected laymen" of his denomination. A state official is convicted of embezzlement and there is a great stir about it in the community. What will be done constructively and redemptively about him in the congregation where he is a "pillar of the church"? Is it a kindness to overlook it? Whom would it help?

Forgiveness must not be viewed as an end in itself, but as a means for providing hope that restoration is possible It is not surprising that little healing came to a marriage in which the husband said to the wife in the presence of the pastor, "I'd kill you if you ever told me you had been unfaithful." Forgiveness was totally missing. But equally unhealed was a woman who for forty years had settled for and enjoyed the "rewards" of her hypochondria even though she had made public confession of her sin before the congregation and had supposedly been forgiven. She had seldom missed a monthly Holy Communion, but she had invalidated its intended healing effectiveness by her unwillingness to amend her life.

Amendment of life, satisfaction (see pages 30 f.), by whatever name one wishes to call it, must be seen as an essential and cannot be passed over in the pastoral use of the Office of the Keys. A female patient in a mental hospital who had been through several rounds of private and institutional psychotherapy, was exceedingly depressed and incapacitated. She finally opened up and told things in group meetings with an honesty that was drastic and novel for her, then she made a formal confession to her priest at the hospital chapel. She was shortly given a home visit. While she didn't return to promiscuity, neither did she use her new freedom constructively. Her irresponsibility continued. She would take a carton of cigarettes with her to an easy chair and watch television all day and all evening. Meanwhile, her laundry, housecleaning, meal preparations and other wifely duties went unattended. Her depression returned and she had to go back to the hospital before the time for her home visit had expired. She later returned home with a new and courageous determination to live more usefully and to fulfill her vocation as wife and mother. Five months later she had another relapse, saying upon her return to the hospital, "I guess I wanted to see how little I could get by with before my depression would return." The prediction was that the validity of her confession would depend upon how she used her life, and that she would have that amount of mental health which her actions and attitudes warranted.

When the writer presented the material for this book as a series of lectures at an interdenominational pastoral-care workshop at Pacoima Lutheran Memorial Hospital, Los Angeles, the most frequently raised question in the discussion periods revolved around the question of amendment or satisfaction. The following were typical:

"What should be done *after* the individual has been restored to health?"

"Do we recognize the need for the healed person to invest in service to others in order to assist in making his own cure permanent?"

"Should the church provide 'satisfaction' as an outlet for the 'need to suffer'?" (He no doubt had the pathological masochist in mind.)

"What if there were no possibility of appropriate 'satisfaction?'"

"What could an unmarried mother do following her restoration?"

To respond to the last question first, it seems there would be a great need for asking rehabilitated women of this kind to minister to others similarly tempted or defeated by the same sin. She could invest her time and concern in guiding girls who are in adolescence or early womanhood. She could support financially, and as a volunteer aide, the home for unmarried mothers nearest to her.

We often underestimate the rehabilitated person's intuitive gratitude after genuine rescue. All that may be needed is encouragement, suggestions, and a little guidance. An additional note to the case of the depressed woman cited on page 109, who began getting up and making breakfast for her husband before he went to work, would be illustrative at this point. Her life was so changed that it was noticed by others in the congregation. She was glad to acknowledge that she had been greatly helped in the church and through the pastor's ministry, and that if she could help anyone else in a similar situation she would be most eager to do so. Another woman in the congregation who had suffered depression (and not without good cause) was put in touch with her. These were no strangers to each other, but now their fellowship was on a deeper level. It was a great help to the second woman, first, to know she was not all alone (as in the hypothetical congregation of 1,000 hypocritical members in Chapter 1), and secondly, to know that there was a "way out." She desired, almost hurriedly, to enter into a confessional relationship with the pastor and be restored to God, society (not least of which were her husband, from whom she had cut herself off sexually, and her child, whom she had been unable to take care of) and her own integrity.

A man, after a couple of decades of duplicity and long

separation from his church, where he had earlier taken communion regularly but in vain, was freed of his guilt. He said,
"I don't know how I can ever repay you; I guess I can't. The
only thing I can do is to help someone else." He became a
"sponsor" for another alcoholic after joining Alcoholics
Anonymous, and even though the other man was not ready
to "go all the way with the program," the intense investment
of time (finding the other alcoholic a job, getting him out of
jail twice, etc., etc.) served the purpose of prolonged therapy
for the first man. He and his wife made themselves available
for extensive work with another couple whose home was on
the verge of breaking up. Although this man had been highly
active in civic work before, his present "works of mercy"
proceeded from a different motivation—gratitude for his own
rescue. As long as he continues to live in service and openness,
his prospects for an abundant life are good.

These examples are not intended to be neat little "success
stories" in an ethereal or romantic sense. For life is a dynamic
stream of issues, new conflicts, and new problems, as well as
new answers, new victories, and "growth in grace." It is not
postulated that the individuals cited above will never again
have a sad day, or a relapse, what some call "back-sliding,"
but it is almost certain that if they run into serious trouble
again, they will know where to go for help. They have discovered and experienced the essential elements that make the
confessional *functional.*

Pastors Assuming a New Stance

Both in hierarchical and supposedly demo-
cratic types of denominations, the clergy are examples and

pace setters. Their attitudes and practices strongly influence the parishioners' view of the church as a redemptive community. The minister who stacked his empty beer cans in the attic because he didn't want his neighbors to see them in his trash barrel will not be able to preach very effectively on hypocrisy. He doesn't believe in openness in his own life, so how can he believe in confession and restoration to community? There are legitimate reasons for the minister "getting away from it all" on his "day off," but it shouldn't be so that he can do in secret things he would not want "proclaimed upon the housetops."

Professor Mowrer has made an eloquent plea for candor and honesty among psychotherapists and clergy alike. This is essential since sick and distressed people seem to be unusually sensitive to a "phony" or a fraud. They also appreciate someone who is willing and able to be as honest and forthright as they themselves must ultimately become. As Dr. Mowrer has said, in most forms of teaching or guidance, it is assumed that the teacher can do what is expected of the pupil. Perhaps it is part of the problem of unsuccessful therapy that the therapist or pastor expects the client or parishioner to be open and honest about his life while he remains professionally secretive about his own. Perhaps there are therapists who use the "client-centered" approach to counseling because they hope it will serve as a professionally respectable smoke screen behind which the therapist can remain unknown and hidden. The client might well say to himself, "I wish I had such an 'out.'"

Parishioners are frequently relieved to discover that their minister is "human." One wonders why this is such a startling discovery unless at one time or another great effort was taken to create the opposite impression. One Sunday School child was quite puzzled when he saw the pastor emerge from the room labeled MEN. It is necessary for parishioners to believe that clergy are people.

In discussing motivation for entering the ministry, seminarians often become quite defensive when the role that guilt may play in such a decision is suggested. They relax somewhat when they are assured that all who agree will not immediately be dropped from the seminary as suspect. The crucial question is: Has this guilt been resolved? Is it still a plaguing, gnawing, incapacitating emotion which will make the minister sadistically judgmental in his preaching instead of ethically challenging? Or is the candidate hoping to solve his guilt by a lifetime of penance without confession and openness? Many a hard-driving worker never finds release from the pangs of guilt because he hopes to get by with only one-third of the treatment—amendment without repentance and confession. What could have been a creative life is only a hectic round of activism and self-justification. In America such a person will be rewarded for his industriousness; however he will probably do as much bad as he does good in the world, and the final balance on his ledger sheet will be little improved. He will still be in debt.

On the other hand, the man who has been rescued from the painful predicament and torture of his personal guilt will know that he has found a solution that is worth sharing with others. He will be like the salesman who believes in his product, not like the one who is simply peddling goods and trying to put something over on the public. A man who has been rescued and now lives in freedom, openness, and eagerness to serve others out of gratitude, has a wholesome motivation for entering the ministry or any other vocation.

The training of pastors will have to take a new direction

if they are to be prepared to use to the maximum effectiveness the resources that their various traditions have developed. Roman Catholic moral and pastoral theology will
have to take the satisfaction aspect of Penance more seriously.
Three "Hail Marys" and two "Our Fathers" or the "Stations
of the Cross" may be excellent devotional experiences and
may deepen worship, but may not be adequate as amendment
of life related to the specific sins of which the penitent is
being healed. Lutherans will have to think more clearly and
preach more biblically about truly *good* works, the fruit of
the rescued life. The discipline of Wesley's method and the
judgment of the early Anabaptists need to be restudied and
applied to contemporary church life.

Training and research go hand in hand. I would like to
see a carefully structured group of eight or ten clergymen
from several different denominational traditions agree to become part of a seminar in which they would assiduously employ the methods which their respective churches have for
dealing with the problems of guilt in their parishioners' lives,
as well as in their own. The seminar would meet at some
respected teaching hospital where consultation with others
on the healing team would be possible. It would take courage
on the part of the medical and psychiatric staff to be open to
such experimental research, for some cherished medical and
psychiatric notions might be called into question during the
analysis of certain case records. But, as has been hinted at
before, surely these notions are, in many ways, open to
questioning.

Prudence as well as courage must be exercised when basic
issues are being tackled. All that is needed to spoil "openness" and honesty is to turn them into exhibitionism. It
would be easy to be carried away by the value of confession

and "help" another person by confessing his sins for him—especially if one had something against him. In spite of the considerable good done by the Oxford Group, there were some serious shortcomings.[1] Some of the excesses could have been avoided by caution on the part of the leadership. This may account for the fact that Alcoholics Anonymous (a spiritual descendant of the Oxford Group) has both "open" and "closed" meetings. It is useful to distinguish between the earnest and the merely curious. A pastor at the workshop mentioned above raised a very pertinent question: "What about the wife to whom the husband has 'confessed'?" A body of knowledge about such problems should be accumulated so that the consequences of this process will be better understood. The present guess would be that confession is still safer than hypocrisy, but this does not mean that there might not be mitigating factors when the penitent's behavior, even with the best motivations, seriously influences the life of another. Questions of the nature of the sin, its frequency, its duration, its social and legal implications, and the identity of others involved all need to be considered under the general heading of virtue, or prudence. The ultimate goal is maximum restoration to God and fellowmen—more than the personal interest of the penitent is at stake. We are admonished to be as wise as serpents but as innocent as doves.

[1] Walter Houston Clark, *The Oxford Group, Its History and Significance* (New York: Bookman Associates, 1951). Another instance of a vital group that struck some snags is the Emmanuel Movement (begun in Emmanuel Episcopal Church, Boston), which suffered from too much publicity and superficial imitation by persons unable to bring it off. It is probable that the approach to the confessional discussed in this book could be spoiled by the same unfortunate enthusiasm. It should become, rather, the normal on-going work of the average parish and not a special movement. The surest way to kill something, no matter how good it is, is to brag about it, call it a panacea, give it a label (e.g. "high church"), and turn it into a popular fad.

The Church as the Fellowship of the Rescued and the Rescuing

The historian, John T. McNeill, reports on how laymen have also labored to rescue and guide lost souls:

> Side by side with this parish ministry of the priestly confessor there has flourished in Russia the work of guidance of a class of devout and spiritually experienced men known as elders (*starets,* plural: *startsy*) many of whom were not in priestly orders, yet exercised an authoritative direction of souls.[2]

Authority for guiding souls is not only given through ordination; it may also originate from *authentic* living. Jesus was not formally inducted into the Sanhedrin, but he spoke as one "having authority and not as the Scribes and Pharisees," who had plenty of formal authority and status. In a modified way, this same principle applies to our present topic.

In Protestant circles there is much talk about the "priesthood of all believers," but often this is mere lip service. Ministers indicated, in reply to question 6 in the survey, that they are handicapped if there is a "lack of a loving group" (see pages 110 f.) in their congregations.

A minister in the pastoral-care workshop cited above asked, "But how do you find the 'rehabilitated' in the congregation?" Perhaps he had not been accustomed to looking for such "elder brothers" because the modern church is highly organized. In his church there is actually an elected office of "deacon." The Board of Deacons is supposed to assist the

    [2] John T. McNeill, *A History of the Cure of Souls.* New York: Harper & Row, Publishers, 1951, p. 311.

pastor in the care of, and generally oversee, the spiritual and social welfare of the whole congregation. But, unfortunately, these men are usually elected on the basis of their being "pillars of the church," respected businessmen, the *good* members. Their recommendation is probably that they have supposedly made no grave mistakes rather than that they have been recently rescued from serious sin and guilt. Such a group of leaders is admittedly needed for many functions in the church, but not for the kind of ministry to distressed persons which we are envisioning here. Those who have not known great suffering are not likely to be the most helpful with the prisoner out on parole, the alcoholic, the adulteress, the lonely and alienated, and those who, rightly, feel unworthy. As Pastor John Simmons said at the workshop, "It's like one beggar telling another beggar where the food is." It's like one alcoholic telling another alcoholic how he was rescued from the hell they both know so well.

We may at last have found a function in the church for which it isn't possible to elect a committee, call in an expert from headquarters for a two-day "training institute," file weekly progress reports in triplicate, and conclude the whole affair with a gigantic rally in the local auditorium. This may turn out to be strictly *individual* work. It should not go unnoticed that Alcoholics Anonymous works very hard to keep formal organization at a minimum.

Begin with one person who has been restored to God, community, and his integrity through the Office of the Keys, Penance, Confession, Church Discipline, or whatever it is called in your church; let him be an elder brother to the next one in need in at least a small way; let him testify to his brother personally and in his own way about how he got off, and then back on, the track, and there will be no condescending self-righteousness, for in one sense they are very much on a par—just at different stages of recovery from similar diseases.

A judgmental attitude will not be a problem between these two brothers. The harshest criticism comes from those who are enslaved by the malady they are judging. Thus an inwardly hostile person may become a pacifist, and a hidebound and *compulsive* spinster may be the harshest judge of the *compulsive* drinker—it is only the external manifestation of their problem which creates the impression that they have nothing in common. However, one who has had difficulties similar to those suffered by the one to whom he is testifying, *but* (and this is crucial) has overcome them, speaks with the judgment of experience. He knows that they both stand under the same condemnation and judgment. It is not one, superior, self-righteous saint looking down his nose at a miserable sinner, giving him a few scraps of advice; it is rather a fellowship of two sinners, with the elder brother, who has discovered the way out of this dark cave, leading the way into the full light of day. "Bear ye one another's burdens. . . ." Perhaps St. Paul was such a successful evangelist because he admitted that he was one of the greatest of sinners. We must find practical ways of implementing therapy by doing away with its greatest hurdle and barrier, namely, *hypocrisy*.

There is no need to wait "till our congregation is ready for this sort of thing." No need to wait for the annual meeting of the congregation to elect a committee of six Elder Brothers. The Elder Brother is unofficially and informally "nominated" when he has been rescued and is "elected" when there is someone for him to help. His "term of office" ends at his own death or when there is no one within his congregation or community who needs to be rescued. This is penance with a punch, amendment of life with teeth in it. As Luther said, a man's whole life should be lived as a "satisfaction." Luther also said that the Christian man is the most free of all because he has now no guilt to *fear;* but, also, he is the most dutiful servant of all and is subject to everyone out of *gratitude* for his salvation.

So ministers and laymen can work together in a priesthood' of all believers. The pastor can find a growing core of persons in the congregation who can share in the pastoral care of those who are in distress, who have been defeated by sin, and who are suffering from the consequences of their guilt; and in turn those who have been helped, can help. Think of what this change of emphasis would mean in a local congregation over a period of four or five years.

Lest anyone fear that this approach will generate a motley assortment of self-appointed junior psychiatrists practicing medicine without a license, let me remind you that there has been no talk of interpreting people's dreams, probing the unconscious, prescribing drugs, etc. There is no need to exclude surgery for those with brain tumors, biochemical treatments for those with endocrine disturbances, or confinement to a mental hospital for those in acute danger of doing violence to others or themselves—the historic churches all recognize that the skills, medications, and compassion of a well-trained physician are as much a gift of God as the Office of the Keys. There is no either/or choice here. This is one of the reasons I would like to see research carried out in fellowship with specialists in medicine, surgery, and psychiatry, as well as with psychologists and social workers.

At the pastoral-care workshop referred to on p. 125, I observed a unique effort in which rescued persons helped others in distress. A demonstration followed the presentation

of the topic: "Family Group Therapy—Is This the Answer?"
by a psychiatrist, a social worker, and a minister who was the
hospital administrator. The approach is still experimental
and draws upon what is referred to as "transactional analysis"
for much of its theory and method.

In the hospital cafeteria, after the usual evening crowd
had departed, there was a quiet demonstration of one family,
who had overcome grave marital problems, ministering to
another family still enmeshed in disastrous conflicts, over the
evening meal. A few simple rules were laid down. Instead of
talking "chit-chat," the conversation would be limited to
more important things than the weather, the baseball scores,
and the usual superficial palaver about the food. As would
be expected, the "troubled" family in the demonstration felt
quite anxious during this role-playing scene because they
were deprived of the usual small talk which most families use
to smother more important issues. Yet, even though the
family playing the part of the "problem family" was, in
actuality, a rather normal family, in less than fifteen minutes
some very significant family issues arose, problems of which
the father in the family needed to be aware.

Later in the week I was the dinner guest of a family which
I had known quite well, but on a highly jocular and superficial level. At this meal things were different. We followed
the above rules and talked about issues that desperately
needed discussion—family relationships that needed attention, the values and goals of some of the children, and the
responsibilities of the father as father in the home—things
that were getting squeezed out in the rush of contemporary
life. For the first time out of many visits, I really "broke
bread" with that family.

Suppose this kind of fellowship began to take place in a

Christian congregation; what might the effect be on family life that was slipping into superficiality and disintegration? Instead of parents playing games of hypocrisy and pretense with their children and children hiding their true selves from their parents or their siblings, openness, honesty, integrity and meaningful communication would develop.

Bold experimentation is necessary to combat the deterioration of family life, the loss of personal integrity, and the value crisis which marks our contemporary American society. The churches cannot help but be involved in finding the most effective ways to cope with these problems. One way is to re-evaluate the powerful resources in the church's tradition for dealing with guilt and alienation; but this does not preclude finding new methods appropriate for healing the distressed.

Vocational Rehabilitation

In Figure 3 (see page 120), we proposed that the true validation of the Office of the Keys or the effectiveness of Penance is determined by whether or not the lost person has been "restored to vocation." Has he rediscovered his true calling and rededicated himself to it? In Table 3 (see page 24), it is stated that "vocation" will be the result of being healed as far as the penitent's personal adjustment is concerned.

It is the writer's contention that the perspective of much classical psychotherapy is not only too narrow but that it stops short at "insight" and intellectual understanding of the dynamics of the problem. Philip Rieff has called it "informative and neutral, rather than transformative and committed [in] character" (see page 41). The Christian Church holds that every man stands under judgment to participate in the world under the Providence of God through some form of work or calling. His life is to be properly stewarded and exercised in service to his neighbor in some way.

Pastoral counseling in recent decades has been patterned largely on classical psychotherapy or its various modifications. Perhaps a better model, if one needed to be borrowed from secular psychotherapy, would have been that of vocational rehabilitation and guidance. Like the physically handicapped, the sinner has also become disabled. He no longer has the ability to live his life and do his daily work as he once did. Guilt causes him to generate anxieties and symptoms that cut down his efficiency. Perhaps for years his life has been ego-centrically directed and warped by hedonistic standards and materialism. He has shirked responsibility with the help of a deterministic philosophy, and floats around in a sea of meaninglessness. He needs desperately to be rehabilitated.

The following steps in the rehabilitation of the handicapped are available through state departments of vocational rehabilitation, the physical medicine departments of large hospitals, and private agencies:

1. *Case Finding* implies going out and making the service known to the blind and crippled as well as treating those who come and ask for help.

2. *Diagnosis* includes a medical history and examination, plus psychological and other tests to determine the extent of the disability.

3. *Surgery* may or may not be necessary to salvage or restore the person to as much wholeness of function as possible.

4. *Counseling* may be needed at various stages along the way to help the person accept the *fact* of his deformity, to deal

with negative feelings of hostility or self-pity, and to keep him from withdrawing into a shell of isolation.

5. *Prosthesis* in the form of crutches, braces, a glass eye, artificial limbs, etc., is provided to supplement the patient's own resources.

6. *Physical Therapy* tries to bring the muscles and other tissues up to full capacity. This is frequently vigorous and taxing. Full co-operation and high motivation on the part of the patient are highly desirable.

7. *Occupational Therapy* relates the patient to reality, to his environment, and re-kindles his interest in activity *per se.*

8. *Vocational Testing and Therapy* directs the patient's attention away from his "invalid" status and the temptations of "hospitalitis" toward the realistic question, "What are you going to *do* with yourself in the future when you are discharged from the hospital?" Insight or self-understanding, alone, won't do!

9. *Vocational Training* may be hard work for a mature man who has to "start over" in an entirely new trade and new way of life. Any *new* beginning is difficult but sometimes absolutely necessary.

10. *Job Finding* is not entirely left up to the rehabilitated person because many industries and businesses refuse to hire the handicapped. Therefore, the government, the Veterans Administration, and private agencies have pushed an aggressive "employ the handicapped" campaign. Those who are recovering need guidance and group support.

11. *Placement* must be made in a position that will use the person's abilities to capacity but not overtax him and cause unnecessary failure. The implication for pastoral care assignments for recovered sinners is fairly obvious.

12. *Supervision and Follow-up* are important because it is easy for a discouraged cripple to give up, stop using his muscles and skills, and sink back into invalidism—"and the last state of that man becomes worse than the first."

Note how in this process the client is carried (sometimes even pushed a little) beyond insight, beyond the path of least resistance, beyond, what might be called in the Church, "cheap grace." He is brought all the way through the dark night of despair and isolation into community and a useful vocation. He can feel accepted because he is now living acceptably up to his full capacity. Whereas he was *dis*abled, now he is *en*abled by a therapeutic process and a loving community to function again.

Naturally it is possible to push this analogy too far, but it seems to convey the spirit which the church indigenously has when its pastoral care of the spiritually and morally disabled is functioning effectively.

The sinner is one who has lost his identity as a child of God created in His Image. He has lost his true vocation, which is to love God and his neighbor as himself, not only in word, but in deed. He has begun to put himself first, in egocentric arrogance and pride. When society tries to bring him back into line with accepted moral standards, he pretends not to be out of step and resorts to hypocrisy. But he may sooner or later pay a heavy penalty for his duplicity. He suffers from guilt in varying ways, and we have seen how disabling guilt can be. He is in desperate need of "vocational rehabilitation," and of being restored to his true calling. The church has wrestled long and developed various therapies to bring about this soul-cure. It has no higher mission than to rescue such lost and disabled persons. A truly functional confession aims at restoring the disabled's integrity and self-regard, returning him to the community from which he has alienated himself, and to loving service in holy stewardship of the life God has given him.

CONCLUSION:
ECUMENICAL CONVERSATION

Ecumenical concerns are currently popular, but there is a deeper reason for espousing this viewpoint. An eclectic approach has the advantage of drawing on the strengths of several traditions without necessarily subscribing to their weaknesses. In the brief survey of the churches' statements concerning the resolution of personal guilt, the unique contributions to an understanding of the process of restoration has been shown. True, some of the differences are largely semantic, but others are distinct insights. There is great need for all churches to re-evaluate their ministries and learn from each other through sharing.

If the term "ecumenical" refers to the *whole* "household of faith," then the pastoral care of the guilt-ridden must be viewed as the task of the whole church, laity as well as clergy. Some suggestions along this line have been made and others need to be explored.

If it is not stretching the meaning of the term too much, "ecumenical" could also imply inter-disciplinary approaches to the genesis, function, and resolution of personal guilt. Universality of knowledge is unfortunately not always present even in our finest universities. A variety of theories about the nature of man and his problems should be given a fair chance in a great university, both in discussion and in experimentation. Rigidly mechanistic and materialistic philosophies must be willing to stand beside other world-views for examination as to their adequacy. A university is no place for the closed mind even if the mind be that of a social scientist.

Conversation implies dialogue, openness, and communication. It is hoped that the reader has seen from the foregoing discussion in this book that the insights of religion, even the theological perspective, cannot be omitted without jeopardizing and seriously distorting any discussion of the nature of guilt and its resolution. Theology must speak clearly, incisively, and helpfully to make its contribution as challenging as possible. There can be no ostrich-like isolationism on the part of any one discipline. The discussion in these pages may serve as a bridge for such dialogue between theology and psychology in the specific and practical issue of personal guilt. In the words of question 7 in the survey, this book should be psychologically as well as theologically "pertinent."

It has not been the purpose of the author to provide a definite answer to the problem but, rather, to raise as many new questions as he has attempted to answer; to stimulate the dialogue among psychological and theological colleagues as well as among the alert laymen in the churches, in hopes that a more functional ministry to the guilt-ridden may evolve. Surely there are many causes of mental illness and suffering besides *guilt;* but where personal guilt *is* the crucial problem in diagnosis and therapy, there religion and psychology meet.

BIBLIOGRAPHY

Barton, John M. T., *Penance and Absolution.* London: Burns & Oates, 1961.

Belgum, David, *Why Did It Happen To Me?* Minneapolis: Augsburg Publishing House, 1960.

Clark, Walter Houston, *The Oxford Group, Its History and Significance.* New York: Bookman Associates, 1951.

The Community of Saint-Severin, *Confession: The Meaning and Practice of the Sacrament of Penance* (translated by A. V. Littledale). Chicago: Fides Publishers Association, 1958.

Dickenson, William Croft (editor), *John Knox's History of the Reformation in Scotland.* New York: Philosophical Library, 1950.

Eysenck, H. J. (editor), *Handbook of Abnormal Psychology* (Chapter 18). New York: Basic Books, Inc., 1961.

Eysenck, H. J., *Uses and Abuses of Psychology*. Baltimore: Penguin Books Inc., 1953.

Frankl, Viktor E., *From Death-Camp to Existentialism* (translated by Ilse Lasch). Boston: Beacon Press, 1959.

Girgensohn, Herbert (translated by John W. Doberstein), *Teaching Luther's Catechism,* Vol. II. Philadelphia: Muhlenberg Press, 1960.

Hofmann, Hans (editor), *The Ministry and Mental Health*. New York: Association Press, 1960.

Keenan, Alan, O.F.M., *Neuroses and Sacraments*. London: Sheed and Ward, 1950.

Killgallon, James and Weber, Gerard, *Life in Christ: Instructions in the Catholic Faith*. Chicago: Life in Christ, 1958.

Latko, Ernest F., *Origen's Concept of Penance*. Dissertation for the Degree of Doctor of Sacred Theology. Faculte De Theologie, Universite Laval, Quebec, Canada, 1949.

Latourette, Kenneth Scott, *A History of Christianity*. New York: Harper and Row, Publishers, 1953.

Le Saint, William P., S.J., S.T.D., *Tertullian: Treatises on Penance*. London: Longmans, Green and Co., 1959.

The Library of Christian Classics: Vol. 14, *Advocates of Reform;* Vol. 20 & 21, *Calvin: Institutes of the Christian Religion;* Vol. 24, *Zwingli and Bullinger;* Vol. 25, *Spiritual and Anabaptist Writers*. London: SCM Press Ltd., 1943-1953.

Luther, Martin, "The Keys," 1530 (translated by Earl Beyer and Conrad Bergendoff), pp. 321-378, in *Luther's Works,* Vol. 40, *Church and Ministry* II, edited by Conrad Bergendoff, General Editor, Helmut T. Lehmann. Philadelphia: Muhlenberg Press, 1958.

Luther, Martin, "The Sacrament of Penance," 1519 (translated by E. Theodore Bachmann) in *Luther's Works* Vol. 35, *Word and Sacrament,* I pp. 3-22, Edited by E. Theodore Bachmann, General Editor, Helmut T. Lehmann. Philadelphia: Muhlenberg Press, 1960.

McNeill, John T., *A History of the Cure of Souls*. New York: Harper & Row, Publishers, 1951.

McNeill, John T., *The Celtic Penitentials and Their Influence on Continental Christianity*. Ph.D. Dissertation, University of Chicago Graduate School of Divinity, 1923.

McNeill, John T. and Helena M. Gamer, *Medieval Handbooks of Penance*. New York: Columbia University Press, 1938.

Mowrer, O. Hobart, *The Crisis in Psychiatry and Religion*. New York: D. Van Nostrand, 1961.

The New Roman Missal in Latin and English by F. X. Lasance and F. A. Walsh. New York: Benziger Brothers, Inc., 1950.

Oakley, Thomas Pollack, *English Penitential Discipline and Anglo-Saxon Law in Their Joint Influence*. New York: Columbia University, Ph.D. Dissertation, 1923.

Palmer, Paul F. (editor), *Sacraments and Forgiveness* (Sources of Christian Theology, Vol. II). Westminster, Maryland: The Newman Press, 1959.

Runestam, Arvid, *Psychoanalysis and Christianity* (translated by Oscar Winfield). Rock Island, Illinois: Augustana Press, 1958.

Selye, Hans, *The Stress of Life*. New York: McGraw-Hill Book Company, Inc., 1956.

Tappert, Theodore, G. (Editor), *The Book of Concord*. Philadelphia: Muhlenberg Press, 1959.

Telfer, W., *The Forgiveness of Sins*. Philadelphia: Muhlenberg Press, 1960.

Terruwe, A. A. A., *The Neurosis in the Light of Rational Psychology* (translated by Conrad W. Baars). New York: P. J. Kenedy & Sons, 1960.

Thurian, Max, *Confession* (translated by Edwin Hudson). London: SCM Press Ltd., 1958.

Tournier, Paul, *Guilt and Grace* (translated by Arthur W. Heathcote, et al.). New York: Harper and Row, Publishers, 1962.

Ungersmaa, A. J., *The Search for Meaning*. Philadelphia: The Westminster Press, 1961.

Watkins, Oscar D., *A History of Penance* (2 Volumes). London: Longmans, Green and Co., 1920.

Westberg, Granger E., *Minister and Doctor Meet.* New York: Harper & Row, Publishers, 1961.

Wilson, Alfred, *Pardon and Peace.* New York: Sheed and Ward, 1951.

'Analytic confession is accompanied by disturbing emotions, whereas in confession to the priest very little or no feelings are involved. one confesses what one prefers confess. there they do not have a 'confess everything'. If they forget a confess something, it is not a sin, they do not have a feel guilty about it. They are given reassurance + absolution'

Sandor Lorand

"Psycho-analytic Therapy of Religious Devotee

Int. J. Psychoanal. Jan. Feb. 1962

Vol. XLIII Part 1

Conflict between ego + ego-ideal is reactivated by the tr., + make analyst a transitional ego-ideal' Freud says pt. us. means + Freud suggest that therapeutic success is only possible "if one can unmask this former object-cathexis behind the unconscious sense of guilt." The Ego + the Id 1927

Conflict arises in intrapsychic is desire for instinctual gratification + rigid moral code which calls for rej. of such pleasures — submission to + moral code to assure protection + final happiness' Early pre-oedipal attachments + frustrations colored + oedipal development + strong emo. charges + responsible for difficulty in resolving + oedipal prob.

Ego ideals exert pressure on S. Ego + ego repressions